CU005488807

Music Therapy with Children
and Their Families

of related interest

Interactive Music Therapy in Child and Family Psychiatry
Clinical Practice, Research and Teaching
Amelia Oldfield
Foreword by Dr Joanne Holmes
ISBN 978 1 84310 444 5

Interactive Music Therapy – A Positive Approach
Music Therapy at a Child Development Centre
Amelia Oldfield
Foreword by Dr Fatima Janjua
ISBN 978 1 84310 309 7

The Individualized Music Therapy Assessment Profile
IMTAP
Holly Tuesday Baxter, Julie Allis Berghofer, Lesa MacEwan, Judy Nelson, Kasi Peters and Penny Roberts
Foreword by Ronald M. Borczon, MM, MT-BC, Director of the Music Therapy Program at California State University, Northridge
ISBN 978 1 84310 866 5

Microanalysis in Music Therapy
Methods, Techniques and Applications for Clinicians, Researchers, Educators and Students
Edited by Thomas Wosch and Tony Wigram
Foreword by Barbara Wheeler
ISBN 978 1 84310 469 8

Let's All Listen
Songs for Group Work in Settings that Include Students with Learning Difficulties and Autism
Pat Lloyd
Foreword by Adam Ockelford
ISBN 978 1 84310 583 1

Receptive Methods in Music Therapy
Techniques and Clinical Applications for Music Therapy Clinicians, Educators and Students
Denise Grocke and Tony Wigram
Foreword by Cheryl Dileo
ISBN 978 1 84310 413 1

Multimodal Psychiatric Music Therapy for Adults, Adolescents, and Children
A Clinical Manual
3rd edition
Michael D. Cassity and Julia E. Cassity
ISBN 978 1 84310 831 3

Music Therapy with Children and Their Families

Edited by Amelia Oldfield and Claire Flower

Foreword by Vince Hesketh

Jessica Kingsley Publishers
London and Philadelphia

First published in 2008
by Jessica Kingsley Publishers
116 Pentonville Road
London N1 9JB, UK
and
400 Market Street, Suite 400
Philadelphia, PA 19106, USA

www.jkp.com

Copyright © Jessica Kingsley Publishers 2008
Foreword copyright © Vince Hesketh 2008

All rights reserved. No part of this publication may be reproduced in any material form
(including photocopying or storing it in any medium by electronic means and whether or
not transiently or incidentally to some other use of this publication) without the written
permission of the copyright owner except in accordance with the provisions of the
Copyright, Designs and Patents Act 1988 or under the terms of a licence issued by the
Copyright Licensing Agency Ltd, Saffron House, 6–10 Kirby Street, London EC1N 8TS.
Applications for the copyright owner's written permission to reproduce any part of this
publication should be addressed to the publisher.

Warning: The doing of an unauthorised act in relation to a copyright work may result in
both a civil claim for damages and criminal prosecution.

Library of Congress Cataloging in Publication Data
Music therapy with children and their families / edited by Amelia Oldfield and Claire
Flower ; foreword by Vince Hesketh.
p. cm.
Includes bibliographical references (p.).
ISBN 978-1-84310-581-7 (pb : alk. paper) 1. Music therapy for families. I. Oldfield,
Amelia. II. Flower, Claire.
ML3920.M89967 2008
615.8'5154083—dc22

2007047294

British Library Cataloguing in Publication Data
A CIP catalogue record for this book is available from the British Library

ISBN 978 1 84310 581 7

Printed and bound in Great Britain by
Athenaeum Press, Gateshead, Tyne and Wear

Contents

Foreword

Haley (1980), one of the original practitioners and writers in the field of family therapy, observed a young man with psychotic behaviour calm down on admission to hospital but return to a psychotic state when visited by his family. Such observations suggested a direct link between family relationships and symptomatic behaviour. Groups of practitioners in the USA started to challenge the time-honoured practice of individual therapy by working with both patients and their families.

Family therapy is now established as an effective intervention in many settings and is an essential component in multi-disciplinary teams. It now seems so obvious to include what is usually the most important context – the child's family – in the treatment and it is easy to forget the struggle of the early therapists to embed these ideas in day-to-day practice.

This book celebrates the fundamental importance of working with the child in the context of the family, as music therapy also embraces the challenge of defying the conventions of individual therapy, in which many of us were originally trained.

All the contributors to this book address the central dilemma of conducting individual work with children. How do we respect the child's confidentiality whilst including parents? A unifying conclusion in all the chapters is the empowerment offered to parents who become a central resource to the change process. This creates a subtle shift in the balance of power from therapist to parent.

Music therapy with families does not mean that traditional skills are relinquished. On the contrary, many of the contributors integrate their therapy with the theoretical frameworks of both attachment and play.

The field of family therapy moves very fast and in the last 20 years there has been a significant shift away from techniques which facilitate communication and understanding between family members to a model that emphasises the significance of how we construct meaning through language. This model, broadly defined as social constructionism, has contributed greatly to our understanding of multiple levels of meaning, both personal and political, which are conveyed through language. However, this fails to acknowledge the richness of information that is conveyed through non-verbal communication.

This book describes how music therapy with families can be an effective non-verbal tool, creating a safe and fun context for communication through rhythm, pulse and melody. Much of the case material demonstrates how music can generate reciprocity and trust between parent, child and therapist. For me, it is particularly pleasing to see music therapists revisiting the principles of many early family therapy practitioners who developed non-verbal techniques such as family sculpting, developed by Duhl, Kantor and Duhl (1973) in the 1960s and popularised by Peggy Papp (1983) and Virginia Satir (1972). These techniques, like music therapy, are valuable for all our patients regardless of educational ability, ethnicity or disability.

Music therapy with families is a refreshing contribution to our work and this book vividly illustrates its application to a wide range of families where children and parents have experienced a range of losses and traumas.

Vince Hesketh
Croft Children's Unit,
Cambridge

Acknowledgements

The editors would like to thank the following people, who have all played a part in bringing this book into being.

- The children and families with whom we have worked and played over the years, whose own journeys have guided our own as therapists.

- The families included in this book, some of whom have collaborated directly in the writing, and all of whom have allowed their own stories to be told.

- The authors, from whom we have learnt much as we have worked together, not least about the human capacity for patience and perseverance.

- The colleagues and workplaces that have supported the idea of this book, and who have often very practically encouraged and urged on the writers.

- Phyllis Champion, for her thoughtful and creative editing which not only facilitates the writing process but makes the experience enjoyable.

Amelia would like to thank her children, Daniel, Paul, Laura and Claire, and her husband, David, for allowing her to continue to juggle work and family commitments, and for remaining supportive and good-humoured through-out this process.

Claire would like to thank Imogen and Maddy, two wonderful daughters, who have been ever-encouraging and uncomplaining as this project has, at times, consumed more of their family time than they might have wanted. And thanks, always, to Steve for his finely tuned blend of support, criticism and confidence.

Introduction

Kay Sobey

With a belated flowering of music therapy publications in the last decade it is perhaps surprising that this is the first to concentrate entirely on working directly with families. Yet this book brings us a range of narratives showing how established such work is and how it has become firmly rooted in every kind of setting, adapted creatively to meet a diversity of situations. The fertile soil which encouraged this and allowed it to flourish has probably been the very nature of UK music therapy where the therapeutic factor of the music is predominantly harnessed through its potential to communicate and to establish relationships between individuals and within groups. We have a therapy here that thinks of each individual not in isolation but as being innately a social being whose capacity to thrive and flourish depends on their relationships with others. As Winnicott (1953) put it so tellingly, 'there is no such thing as a baby…if you show me a baby you certainly show me also someone caring for the baby' (p.99), and it may be surmised that for that baby and carer the very first group experience will be some kind of a family.

Whilst families may have apparently been out of sight in the therapy room they have certainly not been out of mind. Present or absent, nurturing or negligent, they have influenced the child we work with and the way that child will experience their therapist.

The ideal mother, or at least the 'good-enough' one identified by Winnicott, is often considered to have the qualities therapists aspire to offer their clients. 'Mother–infant interaction' has become one of the most ubiquitous terms, frequently cited as informing aspects of the non-verbal relating which happens in the music. As John Woodcock puts it we can see 'an underlying "grammar" behind the therapeutic relationship, the parenting relationship and client-centred clinical improvisation' (Sobey and Woodcock 1999, p.136). These ideas are reiterated in different ways throughout this book, but are explored most fully in Chapter 2, which cites those researchers into early child development who have been influential on music therapists, such as Papousek and Trevarthen. Along with others, these writers found musical terms the most fitting for describing the early exchanges between infant and maternal figure. In the 20 years or so that I have been working in this field there has also been a big increase in the range of work that music therapists approach from a psychodynamic perspective to increase their understanding of the therapy relationships. In this theoretical model the primacy of infancy and the 'first relationship' in affecting the quality of all subsequent relationships is a central tenet. An increasing number of music therapists have now had an experience of undertaking an infant observation along the lines of the model initiated by Esther Bick (1963). Here the focus is not on the physical, cognitive or even communication skills of the baby but on the establishment of an affective relationship between baby and mother (or other primary carer) and also between other members of the family – not forgetting the impact of this on the observer who is privileged to be in contact with them. These experiences provide music therapists with a good grounding in thinking and working with the family as a whole rather than just working with an individual who is presented to them as having particular difficulties.

There is a move to be made, however, from the presence of a maternal figure as an influence on behaviour of either therapist or client to the inclusion of a parent as active participator in the therapy. This is the area about which much less has been written, although in my experience this does not mean it has not been happening. Chazan (2003), in her introduction to a book on parallel psychotherapy for parents and children, talks of a similar situation in that profession. She discusses why simultaneous treatment should have been 'widely practised but not explicated as valuable' (p.13). She speculates that there might be a fear of disapproval when breaking from traditional methods of practice and, as some contributors to this book acknowledge, working with parents has not always been part of a music therapy student's clinical placement experience. This might lead practitioners to avoid public discussion of innovations until their ways of working became more established. Obviously, effective therapy for children has always included the need to establish a good working alliance with someone supporting them, whether parents, teachers or carers. However, even this vital liaison and feedback may bring its problems as is clear from the research at Nordoff-Robbins, alluded to in Chapter 5, which highlights the tension, and potential conflict, between protecting the privacy and confidentiality of the therapy space and therapists' responsibility to the family which make it possible for their child to benefit from this. Horvat and O'Neill helpfully describe the process they went through when they first came to consider bringing a family member (mother or grandmother in their examples) into the room. This felt like an innovation since they had no previous experience to draw on from their training. If this has been the case with other music therapists it may well explain why, with a few notable exceptions, much family work in the past has been undertaken away from the limelight of conferences and publications. We might wonder what was happening in the years between Warwick's research into maternal involvement in therapy with children on the autistic spectrum (published in 1995 but presented as work in progress much earlier) and Woodward's (2004) article on the same topic in the *British Journal of Music Therapy*. Or, the even longer timespan between a group for children with Down's syndrome and their mothers and sibling, run by Jill Moass and Margaret Heal Hughes more than 15 years previously (1994), and the groups described in this book in Chapter 3 and Chapter 4. The seeds sown in this earlier groupwork were, in fact, growing and bearing fruit in a south-west London community team, influencing many fortunate students who were on placement there. This clinical practice, further enriched by collaboration with family and play therapists, remained largely unknown in the wider music therapy world. The work of Fearn and O'Connor (2003), whose article in the *British Journal of Music Therapy* is referred to in Chapter 2, looked back on ten years of co-working when parents were involved in their children's music therapy in a number of ways but this was only first presented publicly at the Tenth World Congress of Music Therapy held in Oxford, UK in July 2002. Meanwhile it had been left to Amelia Oldfield to provide the greatest contribution to the literature and this is clear from the large number of her publications that are cited by authors in this book, as well as by Chapter 1, which so masterfully sets the scene for the rest of the contributions.

The chapters

This book is particularly strong, in a familiar tradition of music therapy literature, for its concentration on real-life stories that are unanimously lively and engaging. Case studies have proved themselves over and over again as the best way of conveying theory – think of Freud or Casement or Yalom: all writers with whom music therapists will have become acquainted in their psychological studies. Like all collections of stories this book may be read from cover to cover or individual chapters can be picked out to suit the many different kinds of reader who may be interested in this field. I am thinking of fellow professionals and colleagues as well as students or more experienced music therapists. Many therapists are drawn to this way of working, although some may find it thrust on them unexpectedly by the needs of a particular family or the ethos of their work setting. Here, this book will be a wonderful resource. Some chapters excel in debating the rationale, reflecting on both the advantages and possible pitfalls, others are particularly useful in providing practical examples of the music-making. Most convey the need for structure and activity as reassuring (for adult members of the family at least) but use more traditional free improvisation too. Many use song-writing and story-telling, one or two with the addition of non-musical 'props': toys, puppets or art materials.

Although some aspects of theories that inform music therapy may become increasingly familiar as the book progresses, they, along with the diversity in the ways they inform practice, ensure that a reader of any chapter will find it self-sufficient. However, each writer brings a different perspective, and reading several, or all, contributions will be rewarded by a deepening of understanding and increased range of practical possibilities. This benefits both those who are looking for ways to incorporate family work into their practice as well as those already doing so, or those who seek fresh inspiration.

The work settings range from the secure base of the Nordoff-Robbins music therapy clinic, through child development centres and an inpatient psychiatric unit specifically for families, to private practice and both mainstream and special schools. I found the latter most surprising and also heartening. Therapy has not always sat comfortably in the educational environment with its abundance of learning outcomes and targets. Nor is it generally very easy for many parents and family members to know they are welcome and included in what goes on in schools. The case study in Chapter 6 (in mainstream education) was, to me, one of the most powerful and moving, and Sarah Howden's argument for the benefits of the school as a setting for this is entirely convincing. The resources made available for the group in a school for those with severe learning disabilities (Chapter 4) were exceptional in providing Rachel Bull with both a regular co-therapist, access to their supervision as a couple and time for additional support work for parents. I am sure these contributions will inspire other therapists to undertake similar initiatives and find arguments to support their case with their employers and funders.

The editors have cleverly found contributors who not only operate in a variety of contexts but use very different ways of including family members in their work: the mother–child dyad might be the most common, but the vivid and touching case examples described in Chapter 7 show us how well music therapy is suited to cementing the father–child relationship, too. Other examples broaden this further and there are mentions of grandparents, siblings, carers and adoptive or foster parents as well as whole family groups. Sometimes work starts with the child alone, moving out to include one or more of the family, but it can just as often be that a child needs family members at the start of therapy and grows to a stage of benefiting more from a one-to-one relationship with their therapist. There is no place for a 'one size fits all' method here and, however enthusiastic therapists may be about including a parent or the whole family in their work, it is also acknowledged that this does not inevitably make it the best solution in every case.

It is not just the family members participating who are diverse, but the way they are thought about and deployed. In Chapter 9 Joy Hasler, for example, is particularly clear that, with the looked-after children in her practice, the member of the family who is caring for them is seen as 'part of the therapeutic team', whereas in other cases the parent–child relationship itself is the focus for the therapy. Again, this reminded me of Chazan (2003), who comments that where there are difficulties of interaction in relationships 'effective treatment involves changing both [parties]' (p.11). As therapists, of course, this is a core belief in that we know ourselves to be part of the change we hope we are facilitating in others. Chapter 2 describes how sensitively this notion may be handled with the families who attend the multicultural community setting. Here, a parent, who themselves could be struggling with communicating in a new language, may not have recognised the need for help with their child and require the gentlest of introduction to the potential of music-making in therapy. Thoughts about subtle modelling, rather than any kind of instruction, are echoed by other writers, as is a central theme of 'empowering' parents and of the usefulness of music therapy in making them more aware of the strengths and healthy aspects of their children, which may be overlooked when things go wrong. This is just one of the chapters to include allusions to Bowlby's theories on attachment and it is no surprise that we have an opportunity to learn more about this from Chapter 8 and Chapter 9, which both discuss the field of adoption. This is a good example of how much can be gained from reading the perspectives of very different personalities and practitioners looking at similar theories and fields of work but from different viewpoints.

Whilst there is great variety in the case material described there are also recurring themes and similar issues are addressed. All the writers stress the need to adapt and improvise, not just musically but in the whole approach to the individual and to the particular family. It was helpful to hear how the familiar practice of groupwork was drawn on in Chapter 5 when the move from one-to-one work was first negotiated into including a family member, reminding us that the family is indeed the first experience of being in a group for every child. These theories are alluded to by others but are articulated and expanded on most helpfully in Chapter 3 in the description of the group with learning-disabled toddlers and their families. As with other writers Helen Loth invites us to think of the very different ways the mother may experience her role through music-making and the complexity of other relationships that such a group can offer. Anyone who has struggled with ways of thinking about this will welcome this thoroughly practical chapter which complements Chapter 4. Together, these contributions offer a rich palette of theories and practices, provoking fresh thinking and choices for those, like myself, who have similar situations. It is notable that these two chapters both describe the more traditional client group at the centre of the work, largely non-verbal children with identifiable conditions that are impeding their development. This contrasts with some of the highly articulate children we read about elsewhere in this unusual collection.

I am aware that this introduction has said little about the major contributions of the editors, which frame the rest of the book. As with many a music therapy session the beginning and end are of particular significance. Amelia Oldfield has characteristically and appropriately given us the grounding in Chapter 1, telling us how she first developed the family work for which she is well known. Claire Flower has movingly described work with those families where a child has reached the end of what is often a tragically short life. In so doing she touches on an area of work that has increased dramatically in recent years, and one where therapists have been most challenged emotionally and practically to improvise and be innovative in the most sensitive of situations. Both writers have turned to the families themselves to tell us of their experience of the therapy and what it meant to them. The inclusion of these experiences (which does occur more briefly elsewhere) is immensely valuable and we can be grateful to parents for providing us with important insights as to the potential impact of our work. Throughout the book personal intimate stories have been recounted. For that reason, in addition to obtaining necessary permissions to use the material, contributors have been careful to change names and disguise identities. It is of special note that, for those families who faced the ultimate reality of a life coming to an end, such anonymity was no longer sought. On the contrary, the families with whom Claire Flower worked were clear that real names be used throughout, perhaps, as she said, as a testament to the children whose characters remain alive and present within their families.

Over and over again I was reminded of my own experience of undertaking infant observation (possibly also that of being mother and grandmother) and the wise words, previously quoted in Sobey and Woodcock (1999, p.135), of Esther Bick (1963) who wrote that we should 'discard fixed notions about right and wrong handling'; but think about 'the uniqueness of each couple' for, she continues, 'each baby develops at its own pace and relates to its mother in its own way' – as does, of course, each music therapist.

Chapter 1

Working in Partnership and Supporting Parents
Music Therapy for Pre-school Children and their Parents at a Child Development Centre

Amelia Oldfield

Introduction

It took me 17 years to realise that it would be beneficial to include parents in individual music therapy sessions with their children. In my work at the Child Development Centre I had always made a point of talking to parents after music therapy sessions with individual children and had felt it was important to be open and clear with them about the work that I was doing. There was already a feeling of working in partnership with parents during this period, but this did not extend to working jointly with them and their children in music therapy sessions. The realisation that parents could work with me in the music therapy room occurred by accident when John, a very determined boy of two, made it clear that he was not going to come into the room with me unless his mother came too. After two years of weekly sessions with the two of them, John's mother, Anna, wrote about her experience in music therapy:

> I remember thinking that it was a good thing that John hadn't wanted to stay in the room without me. It was a delight to be able to see John, who usually took no notice of anyone or anything for any length of time, become totally engrossed in making sounds and music. His enthusiasm and pleasure were so intense that it was impossible not to

feel happy myself, especially when he started to share his enjoyment with me, bringing me instruments to look at or rushing up to me to give me an excited hug. (Jones and Oldfield 1999, p.168)

Since my work with John and Anna it has become routine for me to work with parents and children together. Younger siblings and sometimes grand-parents also take part. Over the past ten years I have seen many advantages to working with families, and have settled into this way of working to the extent that I am now slightly lost when for some reason I work alone with a pre-school child. One part of my brain is automatically focused on the parent and the parent's needs, and at the same time, I have come to depend on the parent as a working partner.

In this chapter, I will explore and examine my recent work with two very different families that had music therapy sessions over a period of 17 months and two years. I describe the families in initial sessions, in the middle of the treatment and towards the end of our work together. Both mothers have written about their perceptions of the music therapy sessions and I will include this material in the chapter. I gave the two mothers the questionnaire included at the end of this chapter (see pp.35–36) to assist them in their writing. I will then describe some of the reasons why I feel it is beneficial to include a parent (or carer) in music therapy work with pre-school children.

The setting

The Child Development Centre, where the work described in this chapter takes place, is an outpatient centre attached to Addenbrookes General Hospital, Cambridge. Children of all ages with a wide range of difficulties will be referred, usually by their general practitioner (GP) or by another medical specialist. The majority of children will be referred before they are two years old. Initially children are assessed and diagnosed by paediatricians, who might recommend further medical investigations or other assessments by the clinical psychologist, the physiotherapist or the occupational therapist. Once a diagnosis is reached, the child and the family may then be referred to a variety of professionals there for regular weekly group or individual treatment.

I first started working as a music therapist at the Child Development Centre for a few hours a week in 1980. The hours have gradually increased and, since 2003, my colleague, Emma Davies, and I both work at the Centre for one day a week.

Music therapy referrals come from other Centre staff who have already assessed and treated the referred child. We treat children with a wide range of difficulties either individually or in groups. However, over the past 15 years the majority of referrals have been for children with communication difficulties, many of whom have been on the autistic spectrum.

When I started working at the Centre in 1980 this was the only specific music therapy post for children in the Cambridgeshire area. Twenty-eight years later, there are now eight music therapists working with children in schools (mainstream and special schools). Since this increase in the music therapy provision, our work at the Centre has been focused mainly on pre-school children. Once the children reach school-age they can be referred on to one of our colleagues working in special schools or mainstream primary schools in Cambridge. This means that we will usually treat children for no more than 18 months to two years before they start attending school.

Gearing up

As I select instruments and put out the appropriate-sized chairs in preparation for inviting the family into the music therapy room, I glance at the clock and listen to the sounds in the waiting room. I am conscious that Heather and her two children, Nick (three) and Jenny (two), have travelled with a volunteer driver for an hour to get to the Centre and I don't want to keep them waiting too long. However, Heather is very calm, as she has appeared to be for each of the five sessions she has attended so far, and the three of them come in and sit down quietly. The children are dressed with obvious care. As we start Nick wriggles happily as I begin singing the 'Hello' song and there is a twinkle in Jenny's eye. I am struck by how united the three of them are as a family, and I am full of admiration for the sense of acceptance and peace that comes from Heather. I remember how difficult it was leaving the house with several pre-school children of my own and marvel at Heather's ability not to appear flustered in any way. I reflect that it seems to be working well to include Jenny in the sessions with her brother, a decision that was taken initially because Heather was not able to arrange for her to be looked after by anyone else during these sessions.

Later in the morning I work with Gina and her son, Luke, who is two and a half. They have been coming to see me for four weeks. Luke has two sisters, one older and one younger, but neither of his sisters takes part in the music therapy sessions. I assume that Luke's older sister is at school and that Luke's younger sister is being looked after by someone else on Thursday mornings. Gina sometimes mentions that they must go and collect her after they leave the Centre, but I have never met her and the question of whether she should attend the sessions with Luke has never come up.

Luke runs in, beams at me, picks up a beater, plays the drum, then turns around and uses the beater to play the table. He then runs to some closed metal cupboards and plays them with the beaters. I encourage Luke to come and sit down with his mum, Gina, for the 'Hello song' and he shouts 'no', continuing his drumming around the room. Gina talks to Luke and asks him to come and join us, pointing out that his special red chair is right next to hers. He screams 'no' and flings himself on the floor in a rage. I look at Gina and reassure her, saying, 'Don't worry, we'll just wait quietly, I'm sure Luke will come and sit with us soon.' After a few minutes, Gina gets up and goes over to Luke who is now lying face down, screaming on a mat and gives him a reassuring hug and takes his hand, gently guiding him to his red chair. He sits down and I play the 'Hello' song and Luke grins widely at me, tapping the guitar energetically, his previous intense protest apparently forgotten. After about a minute he tries to get up, and I say, 'Well done Luke, let's finish on the guitar, one, two, three, finish' as he leaps up and rushes over to tap the metal cupboard with his hands. Gina follows him and joins in with his playing and there is a great sense of energy and fun between them.

I am aware that both Heather and Gina have to work hard to bring their sons to the music therapy sessions. Heather has a long journey and a younger toddler to get ready as well as Nick, and Gina has gently to help Luke over many stuck moments involving loud and vociferous protests. I am touched by the fact that they are willing to make this effort to come to music therapy sessions, but also feel the responsibility of providing an experience that is worth this effort, and is beneficial in some way.

Early years

Nick and Luke's early years

Nick was Heather's first child and this is what she wrote about him as a baby.

> Initially we had no concerns about Nick. I suppose we were simply inexperienced parents. It hadn't occurred to us that for example Nick was late in smiling or crawling, or in fact that it was taking longer for him to reach all the other developmental milestones than he should be.

In the beginning Nick was a demanding baby – but then aren't they all. He suffered very badly with colic and I would spend what seemed like many hours in the evening walking up and down the room with him to try and soothe his cries. Neither my husband or I felt as if we really knew how to look after a baby. How had the hospital allowed us home with this tiny person who was so dependent?

As Nick grew older he became a very contented baby. He would giggle at toys that played musical tunes. It seemed to please him to press a particular button on a toy over and over again so that certain notes would sound. My husband is musical by profession and it came as no surprise to us that Nick responded so well to music.

Luke's early years were very different. This is what Gina wrote.

The first few years of Luke's life have had some extreme highs and lows. Born prematurely, he spent his first four months in intensive care. When he did not respond to treatment for meningitis we moved into a hospice expecting that he would not survive more than a couple of weeks. The weeks turned into months and it became clear that he would fight on. He developed hydrocephalus and had surgery to reduce the size of his head. He was very ill for his first year but continued to become steadily stronger. We are amazed by his achievements. Things like holding up his head, starting to walk and talk, and feeding himself, have been huge milestones for us. We do not know how this difficult start will affect him but it has become clear that he will not be as severely limited in life as we first feared. He is visually impaired and is delayed in all aspects of his development but is now very active – interested in lots of things and people. His moods veer quickly from very mischievous and happy to blind rage but in general he is very affectionate and loving.

Reflections

In many ways Nick and Luke's early years could not have been more different. In Nick's case neither of his parents initially thought that he had any particular difficulties, but it gradually became clear that he was delayed in his development and was on the autistic spectrum. Luke, on the other hand, was extremely ill from the moment he arrived and was not expected to survive. In spite of these differences both Heather and Gina seemed at ease with their boys, accepting and loving them for what they were, rather than being overwhelmed with anxiety about the things they were struggling with. In Nick's case Heather gradually adapted to his difficulties, but was also able to continue to enjoy the things he could do, such as having fun with his sister and singing while exploring musical instruments or toys. In Luke's case Gina still often seemed astonished and full of wonder by what Luke was able to achieve, even though his erratic and sometimes violent mood swings were not always easy to deal with.

Reasons for referral to music therapy

Both parents reported that their boys seemed to relax when music was playing in the background, and this had been particularly useful for Luke when he was very ill. Both boys also showed a special interest in musical toys, which either make noises or play tunes. Heather wrote, 'Looking back it seems that other toys such as bricks or puzzles didn't interest Nick at all; he only derived pleasure from musical ones'. Gina wrote that Luke would 'often choose to do things like banging saucepans and rattling things against radiators and takes pleasure in the noises he makes'.

Both boys also enjoyed dancing, Nick would follow his sister, Jenny, in a bedtime dance routine, and particularly enjoyed it when his dad picked him up and they moved together in time to the music. Luke would enjoy dancing on his own to his favourite tunes and would sometimes encourage various members of his family to join in with 'Ring a Roses'.

Another point that the two boys have in common is that both their fathers are involved in music. Nick's father is a professional musician and Luke's father plays the saxophone and the harmonica. Although it is not a prerequisite for referral to music therapy, the fact that the two families were actively involved with music meant that it was not surprising that they were both referred to music therapy by the child development consultant community paediatricians.

Early sessions

Heather, Nick and Jenny

Heather wrote:

> Music therapy seemed as if it would be just the thing for Nick and so Nick, Jenny and I eagerly went for our first session. I had absolutely no idea what would happen or what Nick (or indeed any of us) might be expected to do. It was a bit of a surprise when after entering the room Amelia began by singing a welcome song. Were we expected to join in?

Did we have to say anything? Was it OK for Nick to make his own noises while Amelia was singing? It felt that it was never explained how I should allow Nick to behave. Some sessions Nick appeared focused and excited to be there; other times he clearly didn't and was reluctant to try any instrument.

The sense of calm and acceptance that Heather brought with her meant that the beginnings of sessions were predictable and reassuring, as she quietly came into the room and sat down with Nick on one side and Jenny on the other. I thought that they would all three benefit from a predictable structure and that it would gradually become clear through playing and interacting together how we would work together. I wanted the relationships between the three of us to evolve and grow through the musical exchanges rather than through verbal explanations.

However, I also reviewed the sessions with Heather after every one, and I remember her mentioning that she was a little shy about playing music herself and not sure what she was expected to do. I tried to reassure her and tell her that she should feel free to do what she felt was right. There might be times when I would encourage her to play the instruments or guide the children but she could also play at other times if she felt like it.

It was clear to me from the beginning that Nick loved music, had a good ear for pitch and recognised familiar tunes and phrases. This was obvious from his humming and singing, from his responses to expectant silences and from the fact that he would often find the tonic and dominant notes on the piano when I was playing a familiar tune. He would not usually hold on to an instrument he was offered for very long, but would briefly tap or strum a guitar held in front of him and tap a drum with his hands, although initially he was reluctant to hold or use beaters. He was fascinated by the wind-chimes, but this fascination often became a little desperate, with Nick peering at the instrument and frantically playing it with repetitive flapping movements, eventually grimacing and crying. If we encouraged him to move away from the wind-chimes he would show signs of disturbance as soon as anyone (usually his sister Jenny) touched the instrument again.

Jenny was very quiet and shy when she started coming and for a long time did not speak at all, although she obviously understood what I was saying. She seemed to pick up on the predictable structure of the session very quickly and clearly expected me to follow familiar patterns. She would take part in playing with her brother and enjoy being asked to help but would freeze and look away if I paid too much attention to her. Occasionally I felt she had a mischievous glint in her eye. I had the distinct feeling that I needed to give her time, keeping her in mind without appearing to direct my attention towards her.

Heather and I discussed what we felt we should be using the music therapy sessions for and came up with the following objectives:

- to provide Nick with an opportunity to become involved in music-making and enable him to be expressive through his playing
- to encourage Nick to interact and exchange with others through music-making
- to enable Nick to remain involved in activities for longer and increase his concentration
- to provide opportunities for Nick and his sister, Jenny, to have fun together, as well as with their mother.

Although I didn't mention this to Heather at the time, I also thought that it might be helpful to encourage her to play instruments herself, and, in particular, for the children to see her having fun and becoming really involved. It felt like she might enjoy letting go and being loud, and that Nick and Jenny would be surprised but pleased to see their mum having fun and being noisy. In an effort to look after her two children and meet Nick's quite complex needs I wondered whether Heather sometimes forgot to allow herself to have fun.

Gina and Luke

Gina wrote:

> We were very pleased when Luke was referred for music therapy even though we had no real idea what was involved. It soon became clear that the sessions would be about working on behaviour by using a combination of singing familiar songs and music-making activities. Initial sessions were quite difficult because I didn't feel confident about what I was doing and Luke could get very angry. To begin with it wasn't easy to see how we would make any progress – Luke would get as furious as ever – throw things and bang his head on the floor and whizz about hardly able to focus on any one thing. After some sessions when he had been angry I would leave feeling even more exhausted. This was often a reflection on how things were going at home with his behaviour – we

could have weeks where I felt I had no control over what to do to help him calm down and stop doing things like throwing everything in his path. It was always one extreme or the other, though, and Luke's mood could quickly switch to delight. In earlier sessions he seemed to really enjoy dancing to the music with me and this could make him really laugh. He would also enjoy hearing songs he recognised.

Although Luke struggled to remain focused on any one thing for long, and his mood swings were often unpredictable and intense, it was clear to me that he was interested and motivated by a wide range of musical instruments. He enjoyed using beaters on the drums (and any other surface in the room); he liked blowing the reed horns and using the shakers or the woodblocks. He had a good sense of pulse and would play clear steady rhythms. He recognised a wide range of songs and showed he knew the words to these songs by inserting odd words in the correct places. He would respond to endings in phrases and tempo changes by looking up or changing his style of playing. He liked dancing and moving to music, especially when held in his mother's arms. He clearly liked involving his mother in playing with him and was very specific about how he wanted her to play. He had a great sense of fun and humour and loved games that involved movement and drama.

Gina and I decided to use the sessions to focus on:

- giving Luke an opportunity to enjoy music-making, gain a sense of achievement and enjoy having positive playful experiences with adults

- helping Luke to focus and concentrate for longer on any one activity

- helping Luke to accept suggestions and directions from adults

- discouraging Luke from drawing us into conflict

- giving Gina a chance to have positive times with Luke, but also supporting her through the times when Luke was having violent outbursts.

Gina and Luke obviously had a warm and very strong relationship. Gina did not seem to have difficulties matching his huge levels of energy and following him when he raced around the room from one instrument to the next. She would join in with his excitement and joy but remain outwardly calm and firm when he threw himself on the floor or head-butted her, sometimes hurting and bruising her. Nevertheless, I also felt that there were times when she was utterly exhausted and drained. I thought that it would be helpful for her to feel supported and encouraged in her parenting role and perhaps be able to share with me that there were times when looking after Luke was incredibly difficult.

Reflections

Heather and Gina were both pleased and hopeful about being referred to music therapy, but also initially concerned about how their children were 'performing' and the inconsistency of their musical responses. They neither of them knew what to expect and Heather was particularly uncertain about her role in the sessions. Thinking back, I realise that I tend to let the interactions within the music-making shape and determine the way we relate to one another. Perhaps it would have been helpful also to explain a little bit more about my work to Heather. I usually lend a video of my work to parents after my first session, but neither Heather or Gina were able to watch the video because they didn't have the right equipment at home, which may have explained their initial uncertainties.

I remember being immediately captured and impressed by both boys' innate musicality. It was very quickly clear to me that they were both interested and motivated by music and music-making. However, both Heather and Gina were concerned about the inconsistency of their sons' responses, so perhaps I should have reassured them both by making it clearer that the music-making was a means to an end rather than an end in itself.

I had great admiration for both Heather and Gina. Heather, for her calm and warm acceptance and organisation – I kept having flashbacks of frenzied chaos when looking after my own young children – and Gina for her ability to remain warm and positive even when Luke was aggressive and out of control. Again, I remembered feelings of panic and terror when my babies screamed in the supermarket, for example. However, these thoughts also led me to consider that perhaps Heather would benefit from being more forceful and loud, and Gina might want to have an opportunity to express feelings of frustration.

Middle sessions

Heather, Nick and Jenny

Although Nick was often quite lethargic and needed encouragement to keep playing, the clear structure of the sessions seemed to make it easier for him to become slightly more engaged as, for example, he came to expect that he would sit down in front of me for the 'Hello' and 'Goodbye' songs. There were also many occasions when he would become intensely involved in his playing. He would play the drums extremely loudly using one or two beaters (which initially he had not been prepared to hold on to). He used a strong, regular pulse and enjoyed the fact that both Heather, Jenny (with a little help) and I would follow his phrasing and stop when he did. Nick would smile and look around at us with pleasure when he realised that we had all followed his lead and would respond to Jenny's excited giggling by wriggling happily and smiling himself.

Similarly, on the piano, Heather and I would sometimes have to work hard to entice Nick to become involved, helping him to sit up when he flopped down on his chair or discouraging him from becoming distracted by kicking the piano. Nick would respond particularly well to pieces played in the Dorian mode (minor modal scale starting on D). He often played 'D' and 'F' on the piano, would sing little phrases around 'D' and seemed to show relief and pleasure when I played in this mode or when a harmonic progression ended with a D minor chord. When Nick really got going on the piano he would play forcefully and loudly, using both hands and looking very engaged, sometimes perspiring with exertion. On these occasions, his playing would seem incredibly intense and I felt as though his involvement was almost too much for him to bear, as he would begin to look tense and worried and seem to need reassurance from Heather and me.

One of Nick's favourite games at this point was watching the bells fall off our heads accompanied by the singing of 'London Bridge is Falling Down'. During this activity, he was aware of how much Jenny was also enjoying the game, and they both seemed to pick up each other's sense of fun. At other times, when Nick was unwilling to sit down with us, I would improvise a song and follow Nick when he wandered around the room. When I copied his movements, matched his steps by stamping and pretending to run after him, he would usually smile and giggle with delight.

Jenny became more and more relaxed in the sessions. She had a great sense of humour and could be very mischievous, deliberately doing something 'naughty', such as climbing on to a table, to gain her mother's attention. However, she also loved playing the instruments and it was often through her involvement that Nick became interested in playing, too. Her enthusiastic and focused attention meant that we could take the pressure off Nick and allow him to drift in and out of playing when he was struggling to maintain his attention. Nick would also sometimes pick up on Jenny's excited laughter and movements and enjoy running around the room being mischievous with her. I noticed that when Jenny was very involved in playing instruments with her brother she would say a word or two such as 'loud' or 'Bye bye'. Any concerns about her language development that might have been in the background were beginning to disperse.

Heather wrote:

> Nick seemed to relish the freedom he had to be allowed to bang a drum or play the piano however he wanted. There were certain notes/musical phrases on the piano which grabbed Nick's attention more than any others, and by Amelia pinpointing these and playing them back to him he could be drawn out of his world and would communicate through the music with Amelia. It gradually became easier for me to relax more in these sessions and start to enjoy them. It was wonderful to play the drum with Nick, only playing when Nick did and stopping when he stopped – Nick was in control and he knew it.

Gina and Luke

As the sessions have progressed, Luke has come to accept their structure. He will now consistently sit down for two verses of the 'Hello' song and for a 'Goodbye' exchange on the bongo drums. His general ability to remain engaged on individual activities has increased considerably. He will also almost always come to the piano at some point when I invite him to do so. He likes playing different verses of the 'Wheels on the Bus' with me, which we intersperse with free improvised piano duets. He suggests different characters to sing or make sounds about and his favourite are 'the monkeys on the bus', which he suggests to me with a mischievous gleam in his eye. I wonder whether he has heard adults say that he behaves 'like a monkey' and he identifies with 'naughty monkeys' in some way. Surprisingly, the noises that he makes for his monkeys are very gentle and carefully sung 'oh, oh oohs'. Here we get a glimpse of a controlled and sensitive Luke.

In between these focused exchanges Luke and Gina play a variety of different percussion instruments, which we place all over the room to accommodate Luke's need to run impulsively around the room. I accompany their playing on the piano and Luke now seems more aware of my playing, sometimes stopping when I stop, following my music when I accelerate and slow down, and exchanging brief rhythmic ideas. He is still very active and impulsive, but can now also be quiet for a few moments and generally seems a little more relaxed.

A year into the work, Luke still prefers us to go along with his ideas rather than taking up our suggestions; however, he has understood the structure of the session and conforms with it. He also understands that each thing that we do has a clear ending that we prepare for by saying 'One, Two, Three and Finish'. Gina and I have agreed that, if possible, it seems to work best to avoid direct confrontation with Luke. Sometimes we quietly wait for him to join us; at others we compromise, for example suggesting that he can have the instrument he wants after we have done the thing that we have chosen. Luke's speech has developed since we started working together and he is now able to tell us more clearly what he wants. In general we are having fewer battles and furious 'No's and more 'OK then's.

Gina wrote:

> As we went on I felt more comfortable with the environment and the routine of what was going to happen. Luke clearly did too. He began to mention Amelia at home and would suggest coming to see her. It was really exciting when he first started to anticipate what was coming – like going straight to his chair for the 'Hello' song. I think the constancy of the sessions has been helpful to Luke – coming every week, being in the same room with not too many other distractions, and the clear routine of the sessions. All these things have helped to make Luke more comfortable, and over the months he has been able to behave more calmly for longer periods of time. He enjoys making choices about what he wants to do and is beginning to understand that it's not a disaster if he has to wait to do what he wants. As his language has begun to develop Luke seems to have reached a new level of understanding and is generally more willing to accept some direction of his behaviour. His attention span has definitely improved.

Reflections

Both Nick and Luke, as well as Jenny and the two mothers, Heather and Gina, seemed to respond well to the clear structure of the sessions, which enabled everyone to know what to expect, relax and enjoy music-making. However, it was the fact that this structure was flexible, and incorporated the children's choices and spontaneous responses, which allowed both Nick and Luke to feel 'in control' themselves and be creative.

Both boys became more able to focus and concentrate. Interestingly, Nick and Luke came from opposite extremes of behaviour. Nick was floppy and passive and needed encouragement to be motivated to engage with us rather than remain in his own world. Luke was very active and impulsive and needed help to relax and stay still. In their own way they both operated by being in control of the people around them. In music therapy sessions they experienced being in control in positive ways through musical improvisations, while gradually accepting the boundaries of an imposed overall structure to the session.

Nick and Luke both showed extremes of emotion in the music therapy sessions. Nick would become intensely involved in his playing, delighting in the fact that Heather, Jenny and I were all joining his playing, but then sometimes finding this experience almost too intense to bear. Luke showed his usual extreme mood swings and, in addition, let us glimpse his gentle more sensitive side.

End sessions
Heather, Nick and Jenny
In later sessions, Nick continued to make slow but steady progress and became more consistently able to focus for longer on a wide range of musical activities. He also gradually became more communicative. He would smile and look straight at me when I started the 'Hello' song, and would often look up when he recognised that I had imitated or answered a phrase that he had played or sung. He would sometimes sing snatches of tunes and seemed to be aware that I joined him and recognised the tune he had initiated. The big difference was that in most sessions he would now expect both his mother and me to communicate with him in some way through musical exchanges.

Jenny changed significantly in these later sessions. Now completely at ease, she was talking fluently, very much enjoying music-making and no longer content to sit quietly and simply support her brother's playing. Nevertheless, she responded very well to praise and was always delighted to 'help'. However, at other times she would be mischievous and demanding of attention, making it difficult for us to focus on enabling Nick to engage and communicate. Heather and I agreed that it was important to make sure that Jenny felt she, as well as her brother, had 'special turns' in the music therapy sessions. The way we worked in the sessions changed and instead of us all playing together most of the time, I would sometimes play with Nick while Heather was attending to Jenny, and vice versa. About once a month we arranged for the children's father to take Jenny for a special outing while Heather and I worked together with Nick on his own.

The other change that occurred during this period was that Heather became pregnant. This did not seem to change her calm and warm approach in any way. At times, I felt that Heather was a little despondent about Nick's difficulties and perhaps somewhat worn down by Jenny's lively and mischievous behaviour, but she generally appeared to find it easier to be loud and forceful in her playing, to the great delight of both her children.

When Nick was offered a full-time place at school, Heather and I agreed that this would be a good time to finish music therapy sessions. We both felt that ideally Nick would now benefit from one-to-one music therapy sessions in his school and that it would not be beneficial to set up further family music therapy sessions with the new baby.

Heather wrote:

> Nick has certainly benefited from these sessions. He is a very happy little boy who constantly seems to be humming one of various tunes. Music is something Nick really responds to and enjoys; it has been a way that Jenny and I feel we can communicate with Nick and perhaps realise he can communicate with us, too. Nick and Jenny seemed to feed off each other and Nick seemed just as delighted as she was that the three of us could have this time to just have fun together. Ultimately it worked very well having Jenny along to help Nick at music sessions. It seemed that she understood we were helping Nick and became keen to help as well.

Gina and Luke

Luke has continued to make progress in all areas. His concentration has improved and, although he still will sometimes want to finish an activity a minute or two after we have started, he will usually allow his mother and me to encourage him to continue for a little longer. Occasionally he will allow us to 'humour' him, for example giggling with us when we make up an improvised piece of music around his repetitive 'no' answers.

Luke's language has increased significantly with frequent positive remarks such as 'That's a good idea'. He can still protest violently when he does not want to take up one of our suggestions and will sometimes throw objects such as beaters or small instruments in an impulsive way. However, he can be encouraged to pick up things he has thrown and return them to the cupboard.

There are moments, now, when Luke appears more thoughtful and he seems to be able to relax enough to listen more closely to the music and to what Gina and I say. Gina and I both feel that Luke realises that it upsets the people he loves when he behaves in violent and aggressive ways, and that a part of him is upset and cross with himself, which makes him feel even more frustrated and angry. We have continued to have a non-confrontational approach to his difficult outbursts, and tried to praise him and reassure him as much as possible. On one occasion towards the end of our work Luke surprised us both by saying spontaneously at the end of the session, 'sorry, Amelia, about throwing and head-banging'.

In the last few weeks, Gina shared with me that she had suddenly realised that she might quite like to learn to play tunes on the instruments herself. We experimented with a few of these during the sessions and she commented that she couldn't imagine why she hadn't thought of this before. Possibly this realisation might not have occurred had Luke not begun to be a little less needy and more independent himself.

Luke was due to start school after the summer holidays and the school he was going to had full-time music therapy provision. Gina and I agreed that I would recommend that he continue to have either individual or small group music therapy sessions at school.

Gina wrote:

> I look forward to music sessions. It has been more relaxing for me than some other activities away from home because I am not concerned about how his tantrums affect other people and I find it easier to concentrate on what he is doing. Over the weeks I've become less upset when he gets very angry. Being with him in sessions has helped in that we have both learnt ways of dealing with his outbursts that I now use at home and when we are out with groups of other people. It's expanded the range of musical things we do at home and we have a shared language for starting and finishing things in a more orderly fashion. It's great to have a dedicated bit of time every week to spend with Luke away from the competing needs of other family members. We're doing something we both enjoy together.

Conclusion

Heather and Gina were both initially uncertain about what role to play in music therapy sessions, but then later wrote that they looked forward to coming and felt that it was a special time that they valued and could enjoy with their sons.

I felt that my work with both Heather and Gina developed into a partnership where we intuitively worked together during the sessions and then discussed our roles, aims and approach at the end of each of the sessions. A parent of a little boy I worked with previously described the role of the parent and the music therapist in the following way.

> Initially the parent can act as a bridge between the child and the music therapist, the relationship and trust between the child and the parent enabling some form of connection between the child and the therapist. The parent is the child's point of reference. By participating in the session, the child is reassured and knows that nothing bad is going to happen. This will allow the child to start to trust the music therapist and allow himself to participate.

> The success of music therapy somehow depends on the partnership between the therapist and the parent. The parent knows the child. The therapist is a specialist who knows how to use techniques, has seen lots of different children and can draw on her experience. They need each other to provide the best set-up for that particular child: the conjunction of the knowledge of the subject and the knowledge of the child. It needs to be a partnership. (Oldfield 2006a, pp.60–61)

When describing my work with Heather and Gina, I have also written about my own feelings and how these emotions may guide me to support parents in ways that may not appear immediately obvious. Interestingly, both Heather and Gina wrote about these very aspects of our work even though I hadn't dwelt on the fact that Heather might enjoy playing loudly or that Gina might want to share with me how hard it sometimes was to cope with Luke's sudden outbursts. The mutual warmth and respect that I shared with Heather and Gina developed through the experience of working closely together in the sessions and played an important part in our work. It allowed us to work together to address the needs of the children and enabled me to support Heather and Gina.

Questionnaire given to Heather and Gina
Questions to think about when writing
None of these questions *needs* to be answered – if they inspire you, fine – but don't feel they have to be answered. Everything on this sheet is just intended as a help, but don't feel in any way constrained or limited by what I've put down.

- Perhaps a paragraph or two about your initial concerns about your son, the first months/years, daily life with him, his particular strengths and difficulties and also what you particularly enjoy about him.

- Why did you first think your son would benefit from music therapy? How do you use music at home?

- Life at home with your son and your other children. Any concerns about the other child(ren)? What do you enjoy about the other child(ren)? Good moments and difficulties with the children.

- First impressions of music therapy. Any particular concerns?

- What did you feel like being in music therapy with your son?

- Do you think he has benefited from the sessions? If so how and why?

- Do you think your other children (if they attended) have benefited from the sessions? If so, how and why?

- What have *you* particularly enjoyed in the music therapy sessions?

- Do you think it's important to be in the room with the children during the music therapy sessions? Why?

- What do you hope for in the future – if your son has more music therapy sessions in school? In general?

Chapter 2

Back to Basics
Community-based Music Therapy for Vulnerable Young Children and their Parents

Tiffany Drake

Small beginnings: Zak

The drop-in is buzzing with mothers, fathers and childminders with their children, who are painting, playing in the sand tray, sharing a book together or joining in the cooking session. But in the corner one mother sits gazing somewhere into the middle distance, apparently unaware of her child's rather destructive and repetitive play with some cars. Zak's mother, Nina, has stopped trying to engage with her son as he usually moves away from her. She can't bear the rejection any more and it seems simplest to ignore him and let him just get on. Zak, who is almost three years old, doesn't play with the other children, seeming almost oblivious to their presence. After some weeks of the drop-in staff observing this and gently trying to connect with this isolated mother they make a suggestion about some special music sessions for her son. One of the childcare staff offers to watch Zak while Nina is shown the music room. She and I then begin to talk over a cup of tea as the drop-in continues around us.

Although it is hard for her to acknowledge that her son seems different to his peers Nina begins to look around and notice the other children – how they are with their parents, the way they look and communicate and the activities they are involved in. She is aware that Zak seems different but wants to ignore the fact as though it is too painful or daunting and might just go away at some point. This gentle introduction to some kind of support is the very most she can consider. The following week, after some time in the drop-in, she brings her son to the music room as we agreed.

Background to Coram's Music Therapy Service

Aspects of relationship are a key factor in the majority of referrals to music therapy at Coram, England's oldest children's charity. My approach and thinking is therefore underpinned by the centrality of relationships to human life, as reflected by these two thoughts: 'A baby cannot exist alone but is essentially part of a relationship'(Winnicott 1964, p.88) and 'No man is singular in the way he lives his life. He only lives it fully in relation to others' (Keenan 1992, p.277). The children referred to music therapy ar Coram range from 18 months to 11 years in age, with the majority being under five years old. Often the drop-in is the first time the children interact in a social environment. The families using Coram's services are frequently isolated, living in poverty, from ethnic minority backgrounds living in a deprived area of London with no friends or extended family nearby to support them. Many do not speak English and may only access the drop-in after several weeks of home visits by one of the outreach team, who help develop their confidence to go outside the home. The informal community setting enables parents to speak to professionals, such as a child psychologist, without having a formal referral to a clinic, and their first contact with music therapy may be via another parent, staff member or my presence in the drop-in. The majority of children in need of additional support have no formal diagnosis but concerns may have been raised through observations by staff in this non-stigmatising setting.

Once the families feel safe in this environment and realise that there are other families in similar situations, they may join the music groups. You can barely get to the door for buggies on a Wednesday morning when every family in the vicinity and beyond seems to arrive hoping to squeeze in the door for 'Music with Margareta'. My colleague, who runs these popular groups for parents and babies or toddlers as part of Coram's drop-in, is also a registered music therapist. These groups, which are open to any parent or carer and their baby or toddler, are similar in some ways to the 'Sing and Grow' projects operating in Ireland and Australia (Abad and Edwards 2004; Abad and Williams 2006). They focus on interactive music-making involving lap songs, sharing instruments, movement and dance. Many of the parents attend sessions believing that they are fun for their child. This is the case, of course, but in addition to this it is enormously beneficial for their attachment relationship and development of social interaction skills. Basic parenting skills can be nurtured in this environment, including mother–baby play and communication, boundary setting, managing behaviours and feeling states. These can be subtly developed through creative and interactive music, movement and play.

Margareta's observations in this setting may facilitate a referral to music therapy for a child and parent who are struggling to relate to one another, or where development in this or other fields appears delayed. This enables more specialist or targeted support to be provided for children or families where difficulties are evident. Referral to specialised support seems all the more natural and less threatening when the starting point is musical play rather than a clinical referral through a health specialist (Hughes 2006). To address the gap in provision for children and families who may need additional support but not individual music therapy, Margareta and I co-run 'specialist music groups' for up to five children at a time. Most of these children benefit from targeted assistance with communication, social and interaction skills, which can be fostered through a range of musical activities and improvisation. Some children accessing services at Coram are too damaged or fragile to make use of group activities and require individual music therapy. One such child is Zak, who was referred for individual music therapy following concerns raised about apparent delays in his development by staff at the drop-in. The staff also expressed concern about Zak's mother's responses to her child and whether she understood that he appeared to be delayed in his play, communication and interaction skills.

Zak's first session

Zak and his mother, Nina, arrive in the music room and she sits on the edge of one of the chairs. Nina remains perched there awkwardly with her coat done up to the collar throughout the 30-minute session. Meanwhile, Zak leaps around the room trying out everything in his reach, flitting from one thing to the next and discarding an instrument whenever I draw close, rushing off to something else with not even a glance in my direction. Looking back at the video of early sessions I feel as though I am watching a choreographed dance where Zak and I circle one another in a manner symbolic of his avoidant behaviour. This pattern continues for several weeks and I begin to feel something of his mother's despair. There is a glimmer of hope, however, both in her willingness to come each week and remain in the room and in his interest, albeit brief, in the instruments. In these early stages I am conscious of ensuring that the parent does not feel pressurised to become actively involved in the music. Even the most well-intentioned invitation to play might send such a fragile parent into a state of anxiety and possibly resulting in them not arriving for the following week's session. Instead, I welcome Nina as an observer, however passively or actively she might take on that role.

With the fleeting nature of Zak's involvement in the room the music feels sparse, with any phrase being barely more than a few notes long before he has disappeared again. I attempt to speak or sing to him using exaggerated intonation, expression and animation to engage him but this has little impact at this stage. Perhaps Nina did not communicate with him in this usually intuitive way, or stopped doing so as a result of losing confidence because he did not respond to it throughout his first year of life. I notice that her speaking voice both to me and to Zak is flat in its tone and lacking in expression. It is hard to hold Zak's attention and it feels as though nothing has any value or worth. He is even distracted during our simple 'Hello' and 'Goodbye' songs. Perhaps these markers are for me and his mother more than Zak himself at this stage, our anxiety being held by these indications of when a session starts and can stop again. Zak's own sense of timing is so fragmented that even the concepts of a beginning and end seem meaningless. My struggle to connect with Zak is amplified by a sense of him having no connection to anything, including his mother – to whom he seems oblivious.

Little by little Zak's uncontained responses settle somewhat. Gradually, his attention seems to be held by certain toys and instruments, and I notice that a pattern is developing in his dance as he moves around the room between instruments in the same way week after week; first, with some encouragement, the piano, then the doll's house,[1] the horns and whistles, the small percussion box, big drum and so on. I comment on this to Nina and she says, to my surprise, 'Yes, I noticed that too'. It feels to me as though the nature of her presence in the room is also beginning to change. She seems to be relaxing a little and begins showing interest in what Zak is doing.

---

1   The music therapy room is also used by a child psychotherapist and child psychologist, therefore there are some additional toys in the room, including a doll's house. This has proved an important tool in some children's therapy, particularly in their use of stories and symbolic play to explore relationships.

Zak seldom responds to anything I say, but he is beginning to be more motivated by the music and it is this that really shifts the dynamics of interaction. On one occasion, Zak had run into the room and was sitting at the doll's house, moving characters and objects in a rather random way. I asked him if he would come and sing 'Hello' with me. My question was met with no response at all. When I began the song with the piano, however, Zak suddenly leapt up, whooped with excitement, scrambled onto the piano stool beside me and played along with all the energy he could muster. Behind us, Nina, on her usual chair but now with her coat undone, laughed at his joy and delight. The energy didn't stop; once he'd played enough Zak leapt down again and rushed over to a little box full of small percussion instruments, whisked off the lid and rummaged inside for some bells and then a castanet, eagerly proffering them towards his mother, although not allowing her to take them. They looked at each other, a rare exchange, as the song continued. Nina reached into the box and chose an instrument for herself and they began to play together, Nina still smiling and Zak still excitedly making short, accented vowel sounds. These articulations of his delight were the first vocal sounds Zak had made in the sessions. At the very most I had heard a husky whisper before this so the power behind these sounds in themselves showed a new confidence in Zak's communication and enjoyment of using his own voice.

The role of music therapy in reworking attachment patterns

Early infant–parent interaction and communication takes on a musical form of expression (Malloch 1999/2000; Papousek H. 1996; Papousek M. 1996), making music 'a fundamental part of our social experiences from an early age' (Pavlicevic 1997, p.114). In some cases maternal depression and contributing factors, such as social isolation or poverty, other mental health issues, separation, neglect or trauma, mean that the intuitive musical engagement between a mother and infant fails to take place. This may result in insecure attachment and difficulties in communication, interaction, emotional expression and cognitive development in the child (Murray 1992, Murray *et al.* 1996; Pavlicevic 1997; Trevarthen 1999/2000). Music therapy can provide an appropriate opportunity to recreate this vital process of attuning to one another, for both child and parent, through shared experiences of timing, rhythm, pulse, melody and pitch, as should have occurred in the natural bonding process (Oldfield 2006b). Damaged or insecure attachment patterns or early traumatic experiences can be reworked or addressed through musical play, even at this later stage of chronological development (Frank-Schwebel 2002; Lang and Macinerney 2002; Pavlicevic 1997), allowing both participants to experience this invaluable aspect of relationship development (O'Gorman 2006; Shoemark 2005). The journey is therefore equally important for each of them, despite the frequent perception that 'this is for my child'. Research shows that children have a preference for infant-directed singing (typified by higher pitch, slower tempo, warm tone, clear structural cues and simplicity) (O'Gorman 2006) over infant directed-speech (Trehub 2004), demonstrating the importance of musical interaction between child and parent. Adopting these styles of vocalisation assists in drawing both child and parent in to attuning to one another at a level from which they can develop a responsive relationship (Trainor, Austin and Desjardins 2000; Trainor and Desjardins 2002; Trehub 2001; Trevarthen 1993). This was demonstrated in Zak's more animated response to my singing than to my speech, although I used both forms of infant- directed communication with him, as I do in my work with most young children. My singing in therapy sessions generally takes on an emphatic quality in lively playful songs with exaggerated cues for anticipation, phrasing and cadences or a soothing tone in calmer songs or those reflecting feelings of sadness or loss. I pay attention to pitch and tempo to facilitate the child participating in the song, be it familiar, such as a nursery rhyme, or improvised. Simplicity, in both melody and harmonisation, and repetition, are also important in facilitating a connection with both the child and parent. It can be useful to build on a familiar theme such as a song the child and parent both know, to reduce any potential anxiety about 'not-knowing' the music in early sessions.

Imitation and reflection of children's pre-speech vocalisations also form a key part of my musical interactions with children, including those above normal babbling age. This crucial part of communication development may need to be explored for both child and parent. The musical framework and my modelling of it may give them both confidence and permission to engage in this playful communication: again, enabling parents who may feel inhibited to communicate through these types of exchanges with toddlers and older children. The voice is a very personal instrument, however, and removing this playful vocal interaction one step away from such intimate expression may make the difference between an anxious or self-conscious parent engaging in the process or not. Kazoos can be particularly effective for this purpose and allow expressive vocal engagement that can be held and contained by the use of an instrument and encourage vocal interaction where it might otherwise feel threatening (Oldfield 2006b).

Infant-directed speech plays a vital role in establishing and maintaining the emotional bond between the child and mother, and in assisting the pre-verbal child in regulating their emotions. In depressed or absent mothers this universal phenomenon in parent–infant relating may be lost, resulting in the child's communication being delayed or impaired and their emotional regulation and responses being fractured or inconsistent. Reciprocity and imitation in early interaction are fundamental to communication development as well as shared emotional experience. This is perhaps most disturbingly evident in the cases of neglected children who soon stop using their voices to communicate because doing so elicits no response, as seen in children in institutionalised care. In cases where a mother engaging intuitively with her child gains little response from him she may lose confidence or feel that her attempts are inadequate because they are unsuccessful, and then therefore cease to offer such interaction. As this pattern of failed interaction repeats itself, resulting in little or no interaction between parent and child, it may become difficult to identify the initial root of this failed connection. What is important, however, is the opportunity to nurture such interaction again between parent and child; something positive is being done rather than something negative being diagnosed (Hughes 2006).

The musical aspects and foundations of relationships and communication may be restored for children and their parents in fragile, damaged, traumatised or impaired relationships, who have missed this critical stage of bonding and development. This is implemented most effectively in music therapy because musical interaction directly addresses the issue through the very means that can resolve it, without the need for words. The work is not just about the therapist 'tuning in' to the child (Casement 1985), but is also concerned with encouraging that attunement between child and parent through musical interaction which emulates the actual mother–baby interaction that should have taken place (Oldfield and Bunce 2001). This process can evolve in a very natural way as the musical relationship is fostered. It does not need overt explanation but, instead, requires flexibility, patience and observation perhaps more than conscious intervention. Just as most new mothers will instinctively attach to their new baby and respond to them intuitively, so the therapist can engage in a similar way with their client. Capturing a child's motivation for musical expression to elicit spontaneous shared musical interaction can be the key to engaging the parent at the child's level.

Government policy in childcare at the start of the 21st century recognises the importance of sensitive, insightful and resilient parenting to nurture emotionally healthy individuals through childhood and into their adult life (DfES 2004; DoH 2004). It is stated that:

> Good, high-quality, timely support for parents as their children grow up is likely to improve outcomes for children in terms of their health, social and educational development and well-being as well as benefiting the parents themselves. (DoH 2004, p.67)

It is also recognised that parents may need support to be 'confident and able to bring up their children in a way that promotes positive health and development and emotional well-being' (DoH 2004, p.65). Alongside this healthcare initiative the *Every Child Matters: Change for Children* document (DfES 2004) also focuses attention on working with children in context partly by engaging and supporting their parents. The emphasis on 'joined-up working' refers not just to agencies and professionals communicating more cohesively but also how we, as professionals, engage parents and families. If we consider the child in isolation we may be neglecting to tackle the whole problem. This is crucial to us as music therapists and we have a responsibility to adopt these changing standards in policy in our own clinical practice to maintain high standards of specialist provision and to ensure we are achieving the best possible outcomes for our clients. It is interesting how little joint parent-and-child work takes place in current practice in the UK given our understanding of the theory and research that underpins these policy developments and the prominence of mother–infant observation in music therapy training. Had I seen Zak alone I might only have seen part of the challenge he was facing and potentially might have missed the fragility of the mother–child relationship which may have lain at the root of, or been a contributing factor to, his difficulties.

Continuation of music therapy for Zak

The dance shifted from being a duet to a trio after Nina's response to Zak's motivation. She became an integral part of the choreography. For some weeks the trio continued with tentative moments of anxiety or conflict as the uncertainty about their developing relationship was played out. We all had to adapt to the changes occurring: Zak to his mother being responsive to him rather than passive; me to Zak engaging with Nina; Nina to becoming actively involved with Zak and myself as she 'learnt' what to do.

More sustained musical interactions enabled each of us to take time to adapt to these new experiences in the containing safety of mutual improvisation. This might be practically played out through me providing a solid rhythmic bass or ostinato to hold together our musical connection. Musical repetition is an important element of this adaptive phase, just as mother–infant communication involves repetition for the purposes of regulation and reassurance.

Modelling is a useful means by which to draw in parents who may seem reluctant, or lacking in their own self-esteem or resources, to engage in playful interaction with their child. This may help to re-awaken their natural parenting instincts for communicative and playful engagement with their child, which cannot be achieved at a cognitive level of explaining to the parent what they should do (Papousek and Papousek 1997). It may be useful to consider the parent's own experience of childhood and whether they experienced playful and responsive interaction with their own parents to help our understanding of why such modelling may be necessary. Through the child's musical motivations the parent may begin to experience positive aspects of a child they had 'given up on' to some extent. Where a child is delayed in speech acquisition but is no longer a 'baby', inciting pre-verbal responses from the parent, this may result in the parent becoming inhibited or losing their competence to engage at this pre-verbal level (Papousek and Papousek 1997). The child's increasing capacity to engage with someone else who responds to them in these pre-verbal ways may motivate a parent who has lost confidence to try again, particularly if that parent trusts and feels supported by the therapist. Infant-directed speech and 'pre-musical' modes of engaging (Trevarthen 2004) are vital tools for the music therapist in achieving these outcomes. The process is cyclical and each has to adapt to changes in the other. Many of the parents accessing Coram's music therapy service have little perception of their own needs at the point of referral. As with the drop-in music groups, the focus is on the child and, in their minds, usually remains so. Even where children are seen individually there is a responsibility to engage the parents in the work in some way. This can be a sensitive issue, however, and it needs approaching with caution in cases where parents are in their own fragile or depressed states, as demonstrated in the following example.

Engaging parents outside the therapy room: Adi

Adi was referred to music therapy by his nursery so I saw him during the
nursery day without his mother. I always meet with the child's parents
before beginning therapy to gain an understanding of their impression of
their child's strengths and needs as well as a history of their development
and family background. I found Adi's mother particularly hard to engage
during this consultation and was concerned that she seemed depressed and
isolated. She showed little interest in or understanding of Adi's needs despite
the nursery's concern about his delayed communication and social skills. My
frustration at the lack of contact with her during my work with Adi led me to
establish feedback groups for her and other parents that I would otherwise
rarely see. From experience I knew that she would not come if I told her I
wanted to speak to her about Adi; the pressure was too great.

In our responsibility to work with the child in their broader context and
to enhance parents' resilience, confidence and understanding of their child's
needs and development, we may need to find creative ways to engage parents
where it is not possible or practical for them to be actively involved in
sessions, as found by Fearn and O'Connor (2003) in their clinical music
therapy context. Psychotherapist Trudy Klauber (1998, p.105) argues that
'any work with parents needs to be highly flexible and responsive to parents'
needs' and that this might involve 'a slow nurturing of experiences between
parent and child which were not there before'. By inviting Adi's mother to a
group with other parents of children just like him, showing her video of him
in music therapy, and offering her breakfast, I might begin to make a connection with her. She came to the group, along with two other mothers in
similar situations. They each believed themselves to be the only one with a
delayed child who struggled in the nursery environment. Three hours later
the child psychologist, who had co-facilitated the group, and I were struggling to stop them talking to end the session. They continued their chat
outside, consolidating their new-found friendship before heading home.
This nurturing of their experiences as parents and their observations of their
child's positive progress in music therapy, as seen in the video extracts, might
contribute towards a more positive approach towards their child and a rekin-
dling of hope. Engaging parents in this way may enhance the child's
progress in music therapy and, conversely, not doing so may reduce potential
progress (Fearn and O'Connor 2003).

The intention of such groups is mainly peer support yet had we invited
these mothers to a 'peer support' group they may not have come. A group

focusing on their child was different, however, and at last they met someone else whose child did not sleep well and did not meet the usual developmental milestones when expected. They were not so isolated after all. Once parents have attended more feedback groups they may even express interest in accessing one of the parenting courses run by Coram. This network of provision only enhances the work being done in music therapy and meets areas of need which cannot always be met by offering music therapy in isolation, again in response to the call for joined-up working and multi-agency approaches to childcare and parenting. This multi-faceted approach is likely to prove more successful than single-strand approaches for addressing the complex needs of families (DoH 2004; Fearn and O'Connor 2003).

Parents often seem to connect with music therapy before being willing to consider other types of intervention because they have a sense of their child enjoying music. This fact takes on more meaning at Coram because of the predominance of families for whom English is a second or third language. Many of the parents accessing the service do not speak English at all but by being in the room (or viewing the video in a feedback group) they can see for themselves what their child is doing and the progress they are making without the need for verbal explanation. Music, often described in that cliché as 'the universal language', can also enable some connection with cultural roots and therefore facilitate the consolidation of identity in cases where this has been damaged or threatened. It can represent and celebrate our differences in creative and positive ways. This was a particularly important aspect in my work with Dana as described below.

Towards a cultural musical identity in traumatised families: Dana

Dana, like Adi, attended individual music therapy but her mother did not feel able to come to a feedback group. In Dana's early stages in nursery, where she cried, screamed or rocked, huddled in a ball humming to herself or scratching her arms and face, her mother was called in to support the staff in helping her to settle. Rather than comforting this distressed little girl her mother sat in the corner either reading a book or sleeping. The impact of her depression was such that she was not emotionally available to her daughter even in this extreme state. The nursery staff found the family very difficult to engage and numerous appointments that were set up for assessment of

Dana's needs or to support her were missed despite frequent reminders. The one glimmer of hope was that Dana sometimes sang to herself and apparently enjoyed music. In music therapy she presented in one of two extreme states: either shadowing me or being totally unaware of me. I had no sense of Dana as an individual. Over several months, however, she began to develop some play skills and to have moments of spontaneous response to my musical attempts to engage her. Her spontaneous movement to music helped inform my improvisation, which reflected her 'African quality' of an irresistible urge for fluid rhythmic expression. She began using her voice with a strong quality which was evocative of African singing; her identity was emerging. I knew her family attended a gospel church and elements of the session seemed to reflect what Dana might have heard in this environment. Although she still often followed my improvisational phrasing as we sang together, there were elements of her own voice emerging. At this time she also began to speak echolaically, imitating both words and intonation of the speaker, and gradually began interacting with peers at nursery, demonstrating some play skills and increasing concentration.

When Dana moved from nursery to school the positive progress she had made was undone with dramatic impact. She began attacking peers and adults, screaming and crying again and attempting to run away. Although the school agreed that continuing music therapy would be beneficial they were not able to support her actually getting to the sessions. The only practical solution was that her mother should bring her. This may have seemed optimistic so I was pleased when they arrived the first week of this arrangement, and even more so when they continued to attend on a weekly basis.

Dana's mother sat in the room as a passive observer, much like Nina, Zak's mother, in those early weeks. Once again it was Dana who drew her into our play with her own persistence, continually offering her mother instruments despite her protestations and the dismissal of Dana's invitations. Eventually she could resist no longer and took the rainstick which Dana had shoved into her lap and shuffled off her chair onto the floor where we had been playing a simple and repetitive game framed by a simple song with clear anticipatory cues for turning over the rainstick. The parallels with earlier 'mother-and-baby' play here were obvious but this regression in our work was necessary to enable us to begin progressing again.

Soon after this the sessions shifted from my role of modelling positive interaction to being able to become the supporter of the parent–child interaction. Week after week the pair came to their sessions and sang songs from their own culture in a language that was totally alien to me. I did not try to learn the language or the songs. It was *their* music which connected them to each other and to their cultural roots. The value of this positive experience of culture cannot be underplayed in families who have often left their homes in traumatic circumstances, such as at times of war or conflict. The parent's sense of loss, separation and grieving is often present at these moments in working with families and need holding as much as the child's own needs or those of the relationship (Hughes 2006; Klauber 1998). My role was to support the repeating phrases of these songs and to provide the steady rhythmic beat on which the music could rest. This safe base was the foundation on which their fragile relationship could begin to be rebuilt. It was the medium by which they could sustain some connection, develop trust again in one another and experience consistency in their play and relationship, which had been all but lost. In moments where Dana got distracted or her mother forgot the words the simple pulse of my drumming or egg shaker could enable them to continue and to survive potential conflict. Dana's own desperation to sustain these shared moments was evident as she passed her mother more and more instruments as though pleading with her to continue the music. The cyclical nature of the songs they sang seemed to echo her mother's yearning for her home country. As she left the room Dana's mother, whose English was minimal, beamed at me. This in itself was a rare expression of happiness but she told me 'I feel happy only when I sing'.

Music therapy can provide the only space where members of a family are positively engaged with one another at times of fragility or stress (Oldfield 2006b). Often, my aim in working with parents is to make myself redundant. When my role ceases to be necessary the time for therapy to end may have arrived. Once some consistency and security is evident in the parent–child interactions they may be able to continue the journey without my support. This is an exciting moment as it is the beginning of a new and positive phase in the life of the family.

Zak and Nina's journey

Now that Nina's involvement in Zak's music-making and play has become a consistent part of each session the lure of this shared experience seems irresistible. Before Nina has barely got her coat off each week Zak has selected three similar instruments and distributed them between us. As the session progresses he might choose three beaters with soft black round heads that resemble a microphone, instruct us all to stand up and sing at the tops of our voices. As he dances and giggles, and Nina joins in, the memory of the isolation and fragmentation that used to describe this pair seems very distant. It is not just in his lively music and eagerness to initiate the musical trio, but in their very presentation. Nina's neatly pressed red linen skirt, matching pretty sandals and crisp white shirt are evidence of her own self-esteem developing. Some months later she is offered some work as an assistant in the drop-in as the staff have also noticed her growing confidence and her sensitivity with both Zak and the other children with whom he now interacts. There are still challenging times and despite Nina's frustrations she cannot help but laugh when, although he is learning to speak, he mostly uses language to object to things she asks him to do. Whilst this might be a normal stage of development that Zak has reached a little later than some of his peers, Nina appreciates the offer of further support with managing this as the child psychologist joins some of our music therapy sessions. To our surprise Zak not only agrees to the psychologist being present but gives her instruments in an invitation that she should join our improvisation, which she does willingly. Through observation and joint work we are then able to discuss Nina and Zak's relationship, and plan strategies for effective communication with him around matters like bedtime. In her usual quiet but committed way Nina has pursued my suggestion about joining a parenting course and signed up for one of the programmes offered at Coram. The network is doing its job, again, of supporting a potentially vulnerable family in making steps for a more positive future. Simple beginnings made this possible rather than alienating a fragile mother. The need to reach back to the very earliest stages of relating, for both Zak and Nina, could be managed through the playful medium of music at a stage when the idea of a parenting course would have been too threatening. Such a course carries with it the implication that the parent has difficulty in managing their child. A referral to music therapy could be viewed from the 'safer' perspective that the child had some difficulty, which might be addressed positively and creatively rather than requiring invasive or intrusive approaches. Taking the time to foster the emotional bond gently so that child and parent might enjoy each other again and survive the challenges together enabled the journey to begin. In the words of Oldfield (2006b, p.90), 'Music therapy [can] enhance the bond between the parent and the child, enable parents to gain new insights about their relationship with their children, and in many cases improve the quality of life for the child and the parent'. The true joy and fulfilment of their relationship can be nurtured through the very medium by which it could have developed from birth, as parent and child connect with each other in a playful musical relationship.

Chapter 3

Music Therapy Groups for Families with a Learning-disabled Toddler
Bridging Some Gaps

Helen Loth

Introduction

This chapter will describe music therapy groups for pre-school children who have a learning disability and their parents or carers. These groups have been running for several years and are funded by a local charity for people with learning disabilities. What differentiates these groups from other therapy in this area is, first, that the children and parents or carers are in the room, and, second, that we work with several families together. The various relationships and interactions that this membership provides affect the group processes. The focus of this chapter therefore is not on what music therapy offers young children who have a learning disability, which has been extensively written about elsewhere, but is, instead, on the context of working with families together, and how this affects and informs the therapy that takes place.

Working together with children and family members is a relatively small but growing area of work in music therapy. Procter (2005) provides a useful review of the literature in this area and of some of the theoretical reasons for working together with parents in the room, which he notes generally takes place with children of pre-school age. A similar type of group to this, but with autistic school-aged children and their parents, is described by Woodward (2004), who suggests that her approach could equally apply to other children with special needs and their parents, and that both parents and children gain from being together in the session.

The family is the environment in which pre-school children spend most of their time and experience their primary relationships. These relationships affect their development and growth. When music therapy takes place within the family context these relationships can develop and skills may be learnt which can continue outside the group. Although the original referral may have been for a child with learning disabilities, parents or carers may also be in need of support, and it may be valuable at times to attend to the relationship between them and the child. The group allows the therapeutic focus to move fluidly between these areas according to each family's needs at the time.

The group may be thought of as bridging several gaps, such as that between the home and nursery school environment, communication gaps between parent and child, and gaps between parents of the children who may feel isolated by their child's difficulties.

History of the group

This group was started in 2002 and was initiated by a group of parents who identified that their young children with Down's syndrome benefited from music. They approached a music therapist and a local charity, Cambridge Mencap, which provided funding. The group remains outside the statutory services and meetings take place in a music therapy clinic at Anglia Ruskin University, which is set in the heart of the city; this history affects the way the group runs. The charity has a remit to support families and carers as well as people with learning disabilities, therefore a music therapy group for the whole family fits well within its aims. Although the majority of children are brought to the group by their mothers, some come with their fathers, grandparents, any two of these family members or with their nanny. In school holidays older siblings may also join the group. The charity also helps people attend by providing assistance with travel to group meetings or by funding an interpreter. The group is, therefore, very accessible and no one is prevented from attending through cost. For the sake of simplicity, I have referred to the adults in the group as 'mother' throughout this chapter.

The music therapy group

Referrals

Although anyone can ask that their child attends the group, referrals are received mainly from the Child Development Centre Music Therapy Service, and from other services that work with families with young children who have special needs. It is considered important that children are first assessed by the statutory music therapy service and are given the appropriate treatment available within this facility, which may be a period of individual music therapy. If it is felt that the child's or mother's needs would be best addressed through a more social group therapy setting, they are referred on to the music therapy group.

The children have a range of learning disabilities, such as global developmental delay, Down's and other syndromes, cerebral palsy or brain damage. Most have very little or no verbal language.

For children with communication difficulties referral aims might include encouraging them to interact and communicate, both non-verbally and verbally, to experience having their own way of communicating valued and to develop their use of voice through songs and improvised vocal exchanges. Some children will be referred to increase their self-confidence and to encourage them to initiate ideas as well as follow direction. Reasons for referral that can best be addressed in a group setting include the development of social skills such as turn-taking, learning how to tolerate being with other children and encouraging them to interact with their peers and express themselves through the music. For children for whom motor skills are delayed, physical aims may also be included.

Some referrals also include suggestions as to how the mother may benefit from this setting, such as increasing her self-confidence with her child, providing an enjoyable experience for them to have together, learning how to be 'playful' with her child and giving the mother an opportunity to experience a different, non-verbal way of interacting with her child, which may provide ideas for using music at home.

The group

As Darnley-Smith and Patey (2003, p.94) point out, children spend much of their time in groups, be it in the family setting, in school or during after-school and weekend activities. For many children, music is an activity which brings them together in various ways. Similarly, music therapy groups can provide these group learning experiences for children with special needs. All children benefit from pre-school group experiences, but children with special needs may take longer to adapt to social situations and therefore particularly need and benefit from frequently repeated experiences such as those provided in music therapy group work. They may also have had fewer opportunities to develop their independence in group settings because of their individual difficulties. These children can benefit from groups in which their mother is present, acting as a bridge to the child's independent participation.

Some of the children and parents or carers in the music therapy groups attend other group activities which aim to prepare children for the nursery or school experience. These are fairly unstructured and involve various play activities to help the child's development. The music therapy group differs from most of these in terms of the importance placed on the group culture and on the membership, which is a small group with regular participants using music as the primary activity. Within the music therapy group, all the stages of social play can be developed. Sheridan (1999) outlines the types of social play which emerge from infancy through to early childhood in normal development. These she describes as solitary/solo play, spectator/ looking on play, parallel play, associative play, and co-operative play. All of these aspects of play may be experienced within the music therapy group. The flexibility of the musical activities, the improvisation base and the focus on adapting activities to the child mean that the child moves fluidly between different types of play.

Group structure

There are generally three or four children in a group, each accompanied by one or two family members or carers. The group follows a similar general format each week: a greeting song, which includes the children's names individually, and perhaps the children playing the therapist's guitar if they are interested in this. It ends with a 'Goodbye' song, which again is sung to each child individually and the child is given the opportunity to give their own response, whether it is a hand wave, a head movement or a sung or spoken 'bye'. In between these songs a variety of activities is used, including group and individual improvisation, action songs, drum games, musical dialogues using the pentatonic scale and listening to sounds. These activities can be very structured or relatively free, requiring passive or active involvement. They involve pair-work with the mother and child, or the therapist and child, just the children together and whole-group activities. The sequence of the session is not pre-planned, but is led by what is happening in the group in the moment, what is therapeutically appropriate, and also what the children and families choose to do.

Importance of the music

It is the child's enjoyment of music which provides them with the motivation to participate in the group, to engage and interact with others, and to attempt to overcome their difficulties. This is also important for mothers, who rate their child's enjoyment of the group as one of the most important and beneficial aspects of it.

Giles and Annie

Giles and Annie, like many of the children, often became very excited when arriving for the group as they recognised the building and door to the clinic. Once inside the waiting room they repeatedly attempted to pass through the next set of doors to the music room. During the 'Hello' song their individual difficulties and needs emerged. Giles could be extremely shy. One of his referral aims was to increase his confidence in interacting with others. When the group started he would show excitement and enthusiasm. However, when the moment in the song came for him to be greeted personally and to play the guitar he screwed his face up and turned away. He was clearly ambivalent and would reach his hand out towards the guitar, sneaking sideways glances at the instrument and then snatching his hand back when it became too much for him. Gradually, his desire to play helped him to overcome the powerful feelings he was evidently experiencing when attention was focused on him, and Giles managed short intense periods of strumming the guitar strings before retreating to his mother for reassurance.

Annie had difficulty tolerating the frustration of not having her wishes immediately gratified. In the opening song she wanted nothing but to play the guitar, and needed help controlling her excitement and impulsive behaviour. Her enjoyment of the music helped her to control her own behaviour and learn to wait until the right moment in the song was reached and she could have a turn on the guitar herself.

Seeing their children's behaviour develop in this way is very positive and encouraging for the mothers, and affirms the child's capacity to learn.

Some of the children have physical disabilities and need support or special seating to sit or lie down in the group. They may have very little movement or be unable to control their movements. In addition to the musical rewards motivating them to put great effort into holding an instrument or making it produce a sound, they benefit greatly from being with the other children. Although more passive than others, their involvement and enjoyment is evident in the way they watch the other children intently, often surprising the group by suddenly giggling at another child or interaction that has taken place.

Managing difficult feelings

Just as with any parent, the mother of a child with special needs will have complex feelings about their child's abilities. In the group setting comparisons are bound to be made, and a mother may notice more acutely how their child's abilities or disabilities compare to others. It can be very tiring to have a child who is very active and who does not easily conform to what is required of him – who does not join the group and is always on their own mission. It may be hard always to feel loving towards the child who keeps banging his head into your face when you are trying to help him join in. At these times, it is important for the therapist to be aware of these complex feelings and to acknowledge and respond to them in a supportive manner. It is an opportunity for the group members to share their own experiences and frustrations, and to support each other. It is also important to recognise and respect that, for some, unresolved feelings about their child may not be able to be contained within the group and they may choose to leave.

Cultural aspects

The musical basis of the group is particularly relevant to non-English speaking families. Some children have been referred because of concern that they are not having the stimulation of interacting with other children and their mothers are missing out on the support of other families with special needs children owing to their social isolation. A music group is considered easier for these families to participate in than one which has more talking: a lack of understanding of English is not a barrier to participation in the group. Both the children and mothers have quickly been able to understand the activities and to participate equally with the other families. This has had great benefits, as both mother and child have gained confidence and the ability to interact and develop relationships with other group members through the music.

For mothers who speak very little English and lack confidence, various ways have been found to facilitate and encourage their attendance. In one instance the support worker who referred the family to music therapy brought the mother and child to the first two sessions, acting as a bridge between the mother and the group. She modelled being a member of the group by participating, and provided the mother with a familiar face until she felt more confident about attending on her own. Another mother was helped by a translator being funded for the first few sessions. This was an example of the partnerships with other organisations, which the group relies on. The support worker brought the mother and arranged for the charity to fund the translator.

The multiple family group

There are some useful parallels to be drawn between this music therapy group and a family therapy model, the multiple family therapy group. Laqueur (1976) first pioneered the concept of treating a number of families together in the 1950s, working initially with patients with schizophrenia and their families. Subsequently, the multiple family model has been applied to other psychiatric disorders, such as drug and alcohol abuse, child abuse and eating disorders. In this model, families who have a common problem, such as a child with an eating disorder or a family member with schizophrenia, are seen collectively with other families who share similar problems for group therapy sessions. This has been found to be very effective. Howe (1994) lists six 'curative factors' which are more powerful or present in multiple family therapy than in single family therapy. Although the music therapy group is not family therapy, which has different specific aims, these factors are relevant to this work, as shown in the following examples which quote Howe's curative factors and apply them to the music therapy group.

- *Universality*: in a group the family learn that they are not alone; other families have similar problems and concerns.

Some families are quite isolated with their special needs child, particularly if the child's condition is not yet clearly diagnosed. It can be difficult for them to mix with other families in the usual pre-school activities owing to their feelings about their child's difficulties and concerns about their behaviour. Some new mothers in the group apologise to the others for their child's disruptive behaviour, such as not joining in or running around the room. Being in a group where all the children have both some similar and some different problems can be very reassuring for mothers, and helps to give them a different perspective on their child's difficulties.

- *Hope*: the group can give families hope as they see other families learn, change and grow, and as they receive support and encouragement from other families.

The children within the group are of different ages. It can be helpful for mothers of younger children to experience older children who have the same condition as their child doing well. If they are finding it difficult to come to terms with their child's disabilities, seeing how other mothers manage can be encouraging.

- *Empowerment*: as families find themselves able to care for and help other families, they increase their own sense of competence and power.

As the music therapy groups develop, some mothers become more involved with other children in the group and find different responses from their own children. These can be quite positive.

Jane and Felicity

Felicity's child, Jane, tended to leave the group activity and try to play with the other instruments stored in the corner of the room. She would refuse to come back, and would watch her mother to see how she responded, running away if Felicity tried to take her hand and lead her back. We decided to leave Jane where she was when she did this, periodically inviting her to return for an activity. During this time Felicity began to interact more with the other children, who were frequently drawn to her warm and engaging manner. She would use her playing to respond sensitively and enthusiastically to theirs, or do the actions of a song for them whilst the group was singing. This was very affirming of her mothering skills, letting her see that she wasn't an 'incompetent' mother as she often seemed to feel. This also appeared to show Jane that her mother was someone who other children found interesting, and who enjoyed playing with other children. The effect of this dynamic brought Jane back into the group, perhaps jealous of the attention her mother was giving to others, but also showing she wanted to interact with her mother in the group, too.

- *Support/acceptance*: the group becomes a support network where families can feel accepted just as they are – flawed just like all families – and friendships develop between families that continue outside of and beyond the group.

This is important for some mothers, who can discuss and compare their children's abilities and disabilities, share experiences of treatment and advise each other how to access various services and benefits. The time spent in the waiting area before and after the group has become a space for this. Sometimes mothers who meet in the group will go for coffee or lunch together afterwards.

- *Imitation learning*: families learn through identification with other families and through modelling behaviours observed in other families.

This can take place in seeing the different ways mothers deal with difficult behaviours or show different ways of engaging their child and drawing them into an activity with them. Equally, the children watch and copy each other, learning both how to play instruments and how to behave in the group.

- *Experimentation*: the group becomes a safe place to experiment with, practise and get feedback on new skills and ways of relating before using them in real life.

Through using instruments themselves and playing together, mothers discover new ways of interacting with their children. They can learn to listen differently to their children, for example hearing their child's vocal sounds as communication that they can respond to in the music. They can use their child's seemingly indiscriminate banging as a possibility to make contact with them and share in their emotional state. These responses can be taken into the relationship outside the music, and the mothers often take some of the musical activities to use at home, thus giving them more ways to play and interact with their child.

Parents' views

Periodically, mothers are asked to complete a feedback questionnaire (included at the end of this chapter). Results from a recent questionnaire showed that all the mothers felt their child benefited from attending the group in terms of developing communication and social skills, learning to be with other children, waiting for their turn, taking initiative and improving their listening skills and self-expression. Many mothers emphasised the enjoyment their child had from being in the group as the most important benefit: 'the greatest thing is she loves it', 'it's good to see him enjoying something he likes'. Benefits to the mother were rated slightly lower, although they were still positive. Some mothers most appreciated talking to others with the opportunities to exchange information and gain mutual support. Others rated seeing their child do new activities that could be used at home and finding different ways to interact with their child as the most important.

Most mothers felt that their child's behaviour in the group had developed in some way, such as becoming more able to play the instruments and perform the various activities, becoming more confident, and more able to sit and wait. All agreed that the group helped prepare their child for moving on to nursery or playgroup. They identified socialisation, understanding group rules and becoming used to a routine as key factors the children had learnt.

Relationships within the group

Within this multiple family group several different relationships are available to the participants. These include mother/carer–child, child–child, child–therapist, child–another mother, mother–mother and mother–therapist. Each of these offers a different way of interacting, and different uses of music. In the following sections some of these relationships are explored within the context of the group.

Aspects of the mother–child relationship

Mother as secure base

Although I talk here about the mother, these aspects can apply to other significant carers. The mother has an important role to play in the group as the 'secure base' (Bowlby 1988, p.11), enabling the child to 'make sorties into the outside world'; in this case, to gain the confidence and security to participate in the music and the group activities. To begin with, the child may need to sit on their mother's lap. From here, the child can start to play a small tambourine, for example, perhaps with mother holding the instrument. The child is first enticed by the instrument, the look, colour and feel of it, and may put it in their mouth and explore in various ways, including making a sound. The mother helps the child to use it in the way it is intended, to focus on the actions that make music with the instrument – she provides the bridge from the baby or toddler sucking the object to the child playing the instrument.

The group and the different activities allow the child to develop confidence and experiment with how much distance they can tolerate from their mother, and for how long. Some musical activities can be carried out on the mother's lap, for some the child will sit adjacent to her mother and share an instrument, for others all the children sit independently with their own instruments. The setting allows the child to move between their chair, their mother's lap, the floor and other children and their instruments. The musical structure provides the holding framework. If the child becomes a little anxious they can go back to their mother for reassurance, or reach out and touch her before returning to playing. The music engages the child and allows them to move in and out of these different positions fluidly. They are involved in the music, and without noticing it draw away from the mother into the playing. They also become aware of their peers, and how they behave towards *their* mothers.

Mother as facilitator and model

Another important role for the mother is to facilitate their child's playing of an instrument, helping them hold or position the instrument, providing encouragement and praise. In their own playing, they can model the behaviour expected of the child.

Emma

Emma and her mother were new to the group. Having taken a small maraca, Emma appeared fascinated when her mother took a much larger but stylistically identical version of it and played with the group's music. Emma gradually responded to her mother's playing, and a dialogue developed with Emma shaking her maraca in order to get her mother to shake hers. As time went on, Emma became less focused on her mother and turned her attention to the rest of the group and their instruments, more secure now in her own playing and able to begin interacting with the other children.

Mother as therapist

In addition to aims for referral from the referring agency, mothers may have their own agendas for their child in the group. They are very aware of their child's needs and may also be working with them in different ways to enhance their development. Specific aims that a mother may have might be to become aware that others have needs, to overcome their shyness or to use their voice. They will, at times, take more of a therapist role in the group to encourage these. Some mothers use a picture recognition system to help their non-verbal child communicate. They have included the music therapy group within this system, taking pictures of the room and the instruments to use in discussions at home. One mother also brought the system to the group, simultaneously holding up pictures of the instruments as I held up the instruments for the child to choose from.

Mother as observer

A vital aspect of this stage of development is allowing the child to gain more independence. This is something the mother may also have to experiment with: letting their child separate and find their own responses to the music and to the other children. Some activities allow mothers to sit back and observe their child playing with the therapist or the other children. This distance can enable them to notice and enjoy the skills their child is showing in their playing and interactions.

Mother as musical partner

Many of the musical activities involve the mother and child playing in pairs, for example playing the bongos together, or both having a beater for the xylophone. These activities can encourage dialogues between them and often lead to humour and enjoyment in the interactions. The role of the therapist's music can be crucial here, providing a 'holding' function for the mother–child couple. The attention from the rest of the group is also part of the holding environment.

A key task for the therapist is to help mothers move fluidly between these roles, particularly if they tend to focus habitually on just one or two of them.

Parenting styles

During the various activities different parenting styles are evident. One mother may play a xylophone first to show her child what to do and then offer him a beater. Another will sit alongside and continually mime the playing action, as if trying to do the movements for him. Another will take hold of the child's arm and 'do' the playing for him. The motives behind these behaviours are varied. A mother may believe that the child needs to physically experience an action to learn it, or she may be showing the anxiety she feels about the child and his abilities. Mothers may be overly worried about how their child is perceived by others and have difficulty trusting that their child will find his own way. It can be helpful to gain a different perspective by seeing other parents playing with their children in a more relaxed or confident way.

For instance, when given a drum to play, instead of holding their child's hand and beating for them, the mother might discover from observing others that if she waits and listens to what the child does, such as touch, stroke and scratch the drumskin, and then copy and respond to that action themselves, they can build up a dialogue with their child. In this way the mothers are enabled to see and appreciate the ways in which their child is, in fact, participating and communicating, rather than only seeing the way in which they are not doing something 'properly'. The therapist needs to be aware of when to intervene gently and when to suggest to parents different ways of enabling their child to participate.

Some mothers can appear uninvolved, sitting back and waiting for their child to do something, taking no part in the playing. They may need encouragement and modelling of how to bring the child into the activity, to not 'give up' when the child does not immediately engage. It is important to bear in mind that the mother may be feeling unskilled herself, or she may be unconsciously acting out her disappointment in her child. In these instances, the therapeutic work needs to focus more on the mother–child relationship than on the child alone.

Other group relationships

Child–child

As their focus draws away from the mother or the therapist, the child can become more aware of others. This can take the form of reaching out to play on each others' xylophones or drums, or all sharing the large ocean drum and tipping it to and fro between each other. Sometimes more intense interactions can develop.

Simon and Tim

Simon and Tim were sitting in the group together, adjacent to their mothers, who were helping them to play small percussion instruments. The therapist accompanied this with guitar. Simon spontaneously vocalised a few sounds. Suddenly, Tim responded with a similar sound. Simon noticed and made a sound back, grinning as he did so. They both stopped playing and a brief vocal exchange ensued, with 'ah' sounds, and smiles and giggles. The therapist continued playing the guitar quietly, supporting the sounds.

The mothers seemed to hold their breath in suspense, watching, not intervening or responding, and allowing their children to communicate directly with each other and have a 'conversation'.

Child–therapist

Within much of the playing I am responding to individual children. Some structures involve the child in one-to-one improvisation within the general group playing.

Adam

Adam would play in bursts then stop as if it didn't matter one way or another. I would initially keep playing, with mother encouraging him to join in again, keep going with his playing. Then I started to stop playing when he did and restart when he did. Adam quickly began to notice what I was doing and gave a short laugh. He continued laughing each time I did this. The next session he began to control me, making me stop and start by his playing. His laughing increased and he evidently found this hilarious. This became a little sequence that we would do in certain pieces. It was an activity which we had developed together; he would try it out on me by stopping playing and looking at me shyly and expectantly to see if I would respond. I did not always notice, or would not think it appropriate to focus on Adam at that moment. However, he has continued trying this behaviour when we are playing together, inviting me to respond.

One of the major roles for the therapist in this group is to support the mother in her parenting and to support the couple, as demonstrated in the various examples above. Often this is through providing a musical frame or holding environment for them and their playing, such as when they are improvising together.

Conclusion

As I have shown, these groups function on several different levels and can address a range of therapeutic aims for the child and the family.

The specific setting and context of the group is relevant to its function. It is based in a non-medical setting in the community. These children are often seen by several different professionals and undergo many assessments and hospital tests, all focusing on different aspects of their disability. In this context, the value of the music therapy group as a non-diagnostic group, which focuses on the whole child and makes the most of their abilities, becomes very relevant.

The group can be a place where the child is given the opportunity to succeed and to enjoy the experience of being able. Mothers and other family members can see their child doing well and learning new skills. They become more aware of their child's abilities, rather than their disabilities. The group offers different and creative ways for both mother and child to develop their relationship and communication, and to enjoy playing together. The multiple family group offers many benefits, including new learning experiences and support.

As the children become older and start attending school they leave the group. The whole experience, for both child and family, may be thought of as having provided a bridge to this next stage of their lives.

Music therapy group questionnaire

Please answer any questions you feel are relevant and add any comments or thoughts you have.

How long have you been attending the group?

How do you feel the group benefits your child?

(Please underline relevant answers below and / or add your own comments)

Developing communication skills	*not at all / a little / quite a lot*
Learning to be with other children	*not at all / a little / quite a lot*
Developing social skills	*not at all / a little / quite a lot*
Learning to wait her/his turn	*not at all / a little / quite a lot*
Improving listening skills	*not at all / a little / quite a lot*
Having fun	*not at all / a little / quite a lot*
Taking the initiative	*not at all / a little / quite a lot*
Self-expression	*not at all / a little / quite a lot*

Other ways you feel your child benefits:

Do you feel you benefit from attending the group? If so, are any of the following benefits relevant to you?

Different way to interact with child	*not at all / a little / quite a lot*
Seeing your child do new activities	*not at all / a little / quite a lot*
Ideas for activities to use at home	*not at all / a little / quite a lot*
Seeing other parents and children interacting	*not at all / a little / quite a lot*
Talking to other parents	*not at all / a little / quite a lot*
Information exchange	*not at all / a little / quite a lot*
Mutual support	*not at all / a little / quite a lot*

Any other ways you benefit from attending?

Have you noticed your child's behaviour in the group change over time? If so, can you say in what ways?

Do you see differences in how your child behaves in this group to other groups? If so, can you say more about this?

What don't you like about the group?

What would you like to be different or have more or less of?

Do you think the group helps your child prepare for nursery or play group? If so in what ways?

Any other comments about the music therapy group?

Chapter 4

Autism and the Family
Group Music Therapy with Mothers and Children

Rachel Bull

Introduction

It is Thursday afternoon and three mothers have arrived at school for the first session of a new music therapy group. Their sons, Mally, Henry and Iran, all aged six, enter the room. Mally and Henry instantly scatter to different corners as Iran goes directly to sit on his mum, Ella's, knee and she smiles warmly to greet him.

Mally, who has a diagnosis of autistic spectrum condition, begins the session by moving around in an anxious, agitated way. After five minutes he settles down next to a box of instruments and begins, without looking, to take one instrument at a time out of the box, tap, tap, tapping it in a distracted manner before discarding it quickly and moving on to the next. He looks fleetingly at everyone in the room. His mum, Nia, appears unsure how to respond. Jenny, the teacher working as a co-therapist, tentatively goes over and begins to tap alongside him, encouraging Nia to join her. The adults seem careful to avoid getting too close to Mally, both physically and musically. They choose a clave and a drum to respond to his cabassa. From the piano, I match their tapping rhythms, reflecting the quality of their playing, whilst holding the interaction in the context of the group by combining these ideas with the musical and emotional material of the other group members.

Nia and Mally, avoiding eye contact with each other, stay in the same place, playing in a similar way for much of the session. Later in the session, Jenny rejoins the pair as Mally selects a bell. Jenny and Nia also begin playing bells. Mally looks at them both for a sustained moment, plays his bell once more, and then discards it.

In the talking time which follows the music, Nia explains that since Mally could walk, he has never before allowed her to sit next to him for such a long period. Jenny and I feel excited by this, but are aware that Nia doesn't seem to share our excitement. She talks to us of Mally's incessant tapping, saying, 'It must drive you mad.'

Henry, who displays autistic behaviours as part of a general diagnosis of severe developmental delay, spends the music session keeping his distance from everyone in the room. He vocalises throughout the 45 minutes of music. Anne, his mum, goes over to him with various instruments, attempting to gain his attention. He looks at her and then walks away each time. Anne seems tired and sits down next to a xylophone, at some distance from Henry, trying out some melodies, which I support on the piano.

Later in the session, Henry walks over to his mum at the xylophone and begins to jump up and down, smiling and looking at her as she sensitively plays a melody to accompany his rhythm. The interaction is brief but seems important to them both. Henry then wanders off again.

Iran, who also has a diagnosis of autism, spends the music session clinging to Ella, his mum. Ella attempts to lead him to the drum or xylophone, playing the instruments to encourage his participation. Iran joins in for brief moments, but soon seems uninterested. At one point he leaves his mum's lap and explores the room a little, then becomes engrossed in self-stimulating behaviour. Ella follows and attempts to direct him towards an instrument and when this fails encourages him back onto her knee. I notice how difficult it seems for this pair to be separate. Later in the session, Iran goes over to Henry and takes his hands, looking into his eyes. Henry turns away but his mum, Anne, is delighted by this interaction.

Ella makes bubbly, friendly contributions in the talking time, quickly connecting with the others in the room. The 45 minutes of talking goes past surprisingly fast and there are few spaces as the mums seem to have lots to say to each other. Ella leaves just before the end of the session to catch her bus.

It is worth pausing at this point to consider where this group experience has its roots.

The context

The group, which ran for two years, took place in a primary school in London for children with severe learning difficulties. It may be seen as unusual for parents to be involved in an educational setting in this way. However, this is far from being a usual school. OFSTED recently confirmed its outstanding and exemplary status. The school has a long history of supporting the families of its pupils and the head teacher recognises the need to consider the emotional well-being of the students. In this environment, family work of this nature can become a possibility.

A sympathetic setting was a crucial element in enabling the work to develop. Jenny, the co-therapist, is a teacher of nursery children at the school. She was released from her classroom duties for half a day each week to run the group, and was supported in attending joint supervision during school time. For a school to be able to offer this kind of commitment to therapeutic work is rare. However, being able to provide a co-therapy pair to facilitate this group made the idea of working with multiple families in one room feel manageable.

The therapeutic thinking behind the group developed over time working as a music therapist with children with severe learning difficulties. Gradually, I had begun to consider the benefits of bringing family members into music therapy sessions. For some children with disabilities and emotional issues which limit their possibilities of relating to the world, individual one-to-one work is still the most appropriate provision. However, there are children for whom it seems that the way to make the biggest difference to their lives is to work with their primary relationships in the room, providing the space and support for both members of the parent–child dyad to make shifts in the way they relate.

When considering family work as an appropriate provision for this client group, I have found it helpful to explore the possible experiences of a family that has a child with autistic spectrum condition.

The impact of autistic spectrum condition on the family

The nature of autistic spectrum condition is such that parents are unlikely to become aware of the disability in the first months of their child's life. For example, many of the families I work with, who have children at the more severe end of the autistic spectrum, describe first registering concern when their child reached the age of 18 months to two years and failed to develop speech in the expected way. The family may experience a slow process of loss of the typically developing child they had at first hoped for. A delay in receiving a diagnosis could add additional time and stress as the family manages the fantasies and feelings about what is causing their child to behave differently.

Within this picture of a family under prolonged strain, the National Autistic Society (2006) outlines significant evidence that mothers experience a greater stress than fathers (Sharpley, Bitsika and Efremidis 1997; Seltzer *et al.* 2000). Traditional gender roles may play a large part in this, as mothers in our society often occupy the main child-rearing role. Gray (2003), for example, found that the father and people outside the family were more likely to hold the mother responsible for a child's behaviour.

We could consider many other reasons why significant stress in the family seems to be experienced more keenly by the mother: damaged sleep patterns or a possible effect on the mother's career, for example. My own work with this client group has led me to focus particularly on problems with the bonding process between the main care-giver, usually the mother, and her child.

Attachment

In a typical family, where no additional problems are encountered, it is hoped that a strong attachment will develop naturally between the child and care-giving adult. Figure 4.1 (Raicar 2008) shows the bonding cycle as necessary for the emotional well-being of both parent and child.

Raicar's cycle (2008), which flows in a clockwise direction, describes attachment cues, such as crying, calling, clinging to, or smiling at, the attachment figure. As the child cries to express a need the carer responds, learning to interpret the need correctly and to meet it. Both carer and child feel rewarded by this process and can enjoy playful interaction which, in turn, strengthens the bond between them.

The child with an autistic spectrum condition may also cry to indicate they have a need to be met. However, it would not be unusual for such a child to remain unsatisfied by the carer's attempts at meeting their needs. In this instance, the child remains distressed and the carer is not rewarded with positive feelings resulting from being needed. Their playful interaction is then hampered. If this circular process is repeated many times, attachment could be severely disrupted. Carers may find it difficult to continue to

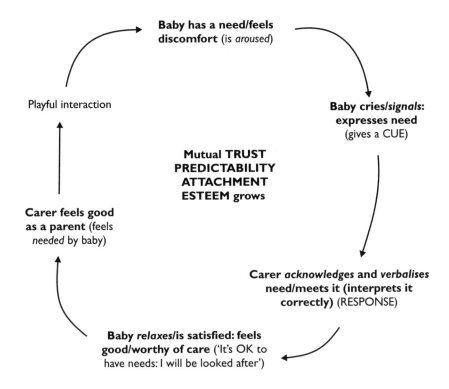

Figure 4.1 The basic bonding cycle (Copyright © Maeja Raicar 2008. Reproduced with permission of Karnac Books)

attempt to meet a child's needs and could perhaps respond by giving up, becoming depressed, or both. Whilst a diagnosis of autistic spectrum condition does not necessarily mean that there will be a difficulty with a secure attachment, this condition is associated with a probability of a less secure attachment than is common with typically developing children (Rutgers *et al.* 2004).

The group described in the opening of the chapter, Mally, Henry and Iran, provides music therapy for the mother–child dyad. The aim is to offer support to both parties, giving them the opportunity to explore their patterns of behaviour in a safe environment. The 45-minute musical improvisation element of the session allows the pair a safe space to try out new possibilities in being together, using a pre-verbal medium to revisit their playful interaction. The music is followed by 45 minutes of talking time for the mothers alone, with the children returning to class. This offers the mothers their own therapy space to bring out their needs and have them met independently of their child. The mothers in our group use this time to talk about their children, but also to talk about other issues in their lives that are preoccupying them. To be heard not simply as a mother but as a person may be crucial in helping the mother find the resources to shift in her responses and to relate to her child in a new way. The following clinical example outlines a relevant shift in the group.

Mally and Nia

Over the next few sessions, a similar pattern continues for Mally and Nia. Mally appears very pleased to see his mother at the beginning of the sessions and they sit together, tapping, for the whole of the music. Session four sees a change in Mally. He begins to play the instruments in a more meaningful way, appearing to pay attention to the sounds he is producing. His vocalising increases and he gives more frequent eye contact as I respond to his playing from the piano. Alongside this shift in Mally's musical persona, he appears less able to manage having his mother close by. However, the moments that they do manage strike me as having a real quality of togetherness.

Jenny and I are both aware that Nia appears drawn to responding as she had in previous weeks, tapping almost distractedly in response to Mally's playing. It feels as if she is holding on to their previous way of relating to each other. The change in Mally's behaviour seems to bring up difficult feelings for Nia, and her anxiety and perhaps anger seems to be communicated through her rather rigid playing, as she sits in a stiff and uncomfortable fashion.

In the talking sessions, Nia describes more of her home life. The family has another child with autistic spectrum condition and both boys have challenging behaviours, neither of them sleeping for more than a few hours each night. Nia has been extremely deprived of sleep for years, but she seems to have found a way to manage this difficult situation. Jenny and I are left wondering if changes or shifts, either positive or negative, are simply too difficult to acknowledge. We remember again in our first session being struck by Nia's apparent lack of excitement when Mally sat with her for a long period.

Following this session, the school breaks up for the winter holidays. On returning in January, the sessions are unavoidably disrupted for two weeks.

Then, before the next session, Nia calls in the midst of a house move to explain that she can't attend due to a painful illness. She feels distant and as if she is slipping away from the work. We decide to run the group just for the boys in order to hold on to some continuity for them. Mally comes into the room and appears immediately aware that his mother isn't present. He spends much of the session seeming happy and content, but not allowing much engagement with the instruments or with the other group members. Instead, unusually, he spends time looking out of the window. Standing close to him, Jenny hears this non-verbal child say 'mummy'.

In supervision, Jenny and I consider the need to hold on to Nia. We wonder if she doesn't expect to be wanted by Mally and that the group may be taking on the same rejecting function. We send a letter hoping she will feel better soon and saying we hope to see her back in the group. She thanks us for our kind words and returns the following week.

Mally looks pleased to see his mum again and repeats his 'mummy' in the early part of the session. Over the following weeks, slowly more shifts begin to happen. In the talking, Nia becomes increasingly open about her feelings, telling us much more of the anger and sadness in her life. She is able to express some of the 'drives you mad' frustration that she mentioned in the opening session. Alongside her ability to explore these emotions, Nia becomes more flexible in her playing with Mally in the music sessions. She, too, appears to become connected to the music she is making, and leaves spaces, waiting before responding to her son. Mally begins looking at his mum for longer stretches and continues to play the instruments in a more expressive, meaningful way.

This clinical example seeks to illustrate the way in which family music therapy can support a mother–child relationship. As Nia uses the talking group in a supportive way, allowing more of her difficult feelings to be heard and acknowledged, so she is able to respond differently to Mally in their music-making together. Through their playful musical interaction, they begin to explore relating to each other in a new way.

Music therapy then offers a useful therapeutic space to the mother–child dyad. However, this pair rarely exists in isolation and is often part of a wider family context. Working with this group of mothers and children has led me to wonder whether providing therapeutic support for the mother–child dyad might, in turn, have a beneficial effect on the family as a whole.

The family context

As each mother will respond uniquely to having a child with autism, so the impact of autistic spectrum condition will be experienced differently by each family unit. When a parental relationship is strong, having a child with a disability can bring a new strength and closeness to the partnership (Havens 2005). However, additional pressures may be difficult for a stressed relationship to bear. Although there is limited research on family breakdown and divorce rates when a family experiences any kind of disability, Hodapp and Krasner (1995) claim most studies agree that there are high levels of marital problems in such families. Looking specifically at the family and autism, the National Autistic Society (2006) cites two sources with daunting figures: Bromley *et al.* (2002), who found that one in three families with a child with autistic spectrum conditions were lone parents, and Broach *et al.* (2003), who found that 17 per cent were lone parents compared to a 10 per cent national average.

It is not difficult to identify the many areas of family life which could come under strain: financial pressures exacerbated by a parent being unable to work; limited extended family support with inadequate respite; challenging behaviours in the child and isolation from the community. In my work with this client group, I have found it useful to reflect on the family's management of the triangular relationship: mother, father and child.

In a typical family the child, between the ages of 10 and 18 months, would begin to invest significant emotional energy in the father and other family members (Smith 2007); the mother–child dyad broadens to include the father, and two becomes three. This important and sometimes challenging phase in any family's life may be influenced by the parents' own experiences of this phase with their parents, and also by the quality of their marital relationship (Pincus and Dare 1978). A child with autism in the family can bring additional difficulties: the child may not instigate a natural separating from mother in the same way as a typically developing child, or the mother may respond by being overprotective of her vulnerable child, finding separation extremely difficult. For the father, it may be hard to challenge his partner and claim time for his own relationship with the child to flourish, as well as time for his relationship with his stressed and potentially unavailable wife. Siblings may also feel the effect of a less available mother, bringing more stress to the family unit.

In the music therapy group, although the focus is on the mother–child relationship present in the room, this relationship is considered within its family context. The mother and child's therapeutic experience is not viewed in isolation but in terms of its ripples through the whole family. In the opening session, Ella and Iran appear comfortable when physically close together. The following example illustrates an exploration of moments of space in their relationship. These moments are brief and appear challenging for both mother and son. However, it may be possible to see some reflections of their therapeutic journey in their wider family context.

Ella and Iran

In our first week, Iran spends much of the music session sitting on his mum's knee. Small amounts of playing are possible, but Iran doesn't seem interested in becoming involved with anything for long. In the talking session, Ella describes how Iran is very tuned in to her moods. She also appears to antici-pate and interpret all his communications very accurately. Ella remembers the time when Iran began to attend school and describes this separation as nearly killing her. As she talks, Jenny and I are struck by Ella's presence in the group. She fills the spaces, engaging everyone in such a way that we both feel pulled to be her friends rather than her therapists. Iran's father is described as 'off the scene' and is mentioned as behaving in a useless fashion. Endings of the session feel difficult and Ella often leaves early or visits the bathroom, perhaps finding it easier to take some control of this boundary.

One year into the work and Ella and Iran have been sporadic attendees, although Ella has always given notice of her inability to attend, and has therefore kept hold of their place in the group. The music session is about to begin. Iran starts the group in his usual position, on mum's lap. Ella takes him over to the xylophone and Iran tries playing some individual notes. In response, also on the xylophone, Ella leaves some pauses in her playing as she listens to her son. Iran then moves to the piano and sits next to me with Ella following and taking her seat on the other side. Iran plays individual notes in a tentative manner and I respond to him, meeting his playing. Ella adds the odd note at the high register which I also try to reflect, and she redirects him when he becomes distracted. It feels more possible to have a dialogue with Iran than in previous weeks. Iran then leaves both of us and goes over to the drum. He experiments with playing in different ways, tapping his fingers gently and then banging the drum more vigorously. Ella does not follow him, but instead moves over to the far side of the room and watches him play. This separate moment in the music lasts for ten minutes.

In the talking, Ella is very open about her difficulties in living with Iran. She explains that he has been very distressed recently and says she doesn't know why. This is striking as previously Ella has only described the 'tuned-in' nature of their relationship. She expresses concern at the needs of a second child and how he may be missing out on her attention. Although he is not talked about in any depth, Iran's father is mentioned in the group and appears to be becoming a little more involved in family life.

In this example, the tentative exploration of a different way of relating is visible through the small shifts in both the music and the talking elements of the session. Although it was challenging for the pair, it was notable that as the moments of space became possible in the mother–child relationship, so as a group we heard more about the whole family.

Families in groups

Having explored some of the thinking behind providing music therapy for a mother–child dyad, the question remains: why work with a group of dyads rather than simply individual pairs? This is no doubt a complex question. I began with an instinct rather than a clear idea of the benefits of groups. However, in the course of developing the model, certain qualities of group work have emerged, such as the ideas of holding and universality that I feel are particularly helpful to the therapeutic process.

Holding the group

In our 'ideal' family, we may wish for a mother and child to be surrounded by a larger family group, providing a context for this primary dyad, and, it is hoped, offering them the protection, support, understanding and challenge that they need. As the mother holds the baby, so the family holds the mother and child. Within this context, although preoccupied with her role, the mother is not only a mother to a new baby, but also a partner, daughter and friend. When things become difficult with her child, these other relation-ships may give reassurance and comfort, providing the new mother with renewed resources in her relationship with the child.

In the music therapy work, placing the mother–child dyads within a group structure appears to resonate with the family model. The pair is not alone, but instead held within a group (family) context. The group can be supportive, protective, understanding and offer challenge. The relationship with the group can offer something extra to the mother, some additional support in relating to her child. In the following example, Anne appears to find support and renewed resources through her relationship with the group.

Anne and Henry

In the opening session, Anne tries many different ways of being with her son, Henry. He gives her small moments of eye contact and then walks away. Henry also responds to other members of the group in a similar fashion. When tired of this apparent rejection, Anne takes time out from trying to be with him and instead sits down and plays the xylophone for herself. At these times I support her playing from the piano, and attempt to convey musically that her playing alone is equally valued in the group. Anne is part of the musical texture at such times. She doesn't take the floor, but her music is held within the musical whole. I notice that occasionally the mothers all make connections to each other in their playing, such as reflecting rhythmic patterns or choosing a similar instrument to play. At other times, Anne takes breaks from playing and observes the other members of the group.

Henry appears to benefit from these breaks in interacting. Perhaps he gains the space he needs to allow a possible connection at a later point in the session. After a while, Anne seems revived and goes back to Henry, trying to find a different way to be with her son. She is then rewarded with moments of joy as Henry uses his bouncing to connect with her and they make music together. Over the months and years, Anne finds the resources to keep approaching Henry in new ways. This on/off approach seems to suit Henry and their moments of connection blossom and become much more frequent in the sessions. In the talking, Anne often offers her support to the other mums through her reflections from her time spent observing.

In this example, Anne and Henry are held by the group. Whilst resting from interacting with her son, Anne is not only a mother perhaps feeling rejected by her child, but is also engaging with other ways of being in the group, such as feeling heard as an individual, connecting with others experiencing similar difficulties, or offering understanding and support to those around her. A group has the potential, like a family, to offer a context, a safe, secure structure within which the mother–child dyad can grow.

Universality in groups

Families of children with autism may experience isolation in their communities. Indeed, there appears to be a greater risk of depression, anxiety and social isolation in families managing autistic spectrum conditions than is found with other kinds of disability (National Autistic Society 2006). The nature of this disability is such that the child may behave in a way that family members find difficult to cope with socially. They may behave aggressively towards themselves or others for example. Many of the families I work with speak of their struggle in managing the reactions of their friends and wider family members when they are confronted with a child who is different.

Providing a therapeutic group for mother–child dyads gives all the members the possibility of belonging. Similar experiences can be identified and a new community can be created. This strength of group work was identified by Yalom (1995) and named 'universality'. The following example outlines how universality can be useful to the therapeutic process.

Mally and Henry

In the music sessions, both Mally and Henry's behaviour could be experienced as rejecting of their mothers. The fact that both women experience this similar behaviour seems to help them move on quite quickly from their possible feelings of exposure at this rejection being on show to the group. Anne and Nia appear to find strength in their similar experiences and perhaps this helps them take risks in continuing to try to make connections with their sons.

In the talking, Ella openly discusses her child's distress. She explains how upset this makes her and the group listens attentively. Nia, who could be described as a more reserved group member, then seems able to share her own feelings about her difficulties with her sons. Recognising the similarities may be helping her find a way to talk about how hard life is and to express her feelings about the trials of everyday life. All the group members acknowledge how impossible they find talking to other friends about issues which are so far outside other people's experience, such as the smearing of faeces. In the group environment topics that are taboo in the outside world may be discussed and feelings around these issues expressed. As one mother talks of despair and rage at her situation, so another is able to face her own feelings that perhaps have been too difficult to contemplate outside the group. Small steps of achievement that may not be so understandable to those with typically developing children can be acknowledged and celebrated. This universality enables the group to be a safe, containing environment.

The model

Although the above strengths can be identified when considering a group for mother–child dyads, this leaves us with the complex picture of working simultaneously with multiple families. In order to provide an appropriate environment, thought needs to be given to the model of the therapy. I have found working with a co-therapist and providing a balance in structure between music and talking elements of the session to be crucial ingredients in creating a safe, containing, therapeutic space. These elements of the model bring their own advantages and challenges to the group process.

The co-therapy dyad

When first contemplating this group, I felt drawn to working in a co-therapy pair; the thought of approaching this large piece of work alone simply felt too overwhelming. Having written previously about the strengths and difficulties of working as co-therapists with non-music therapists (Bull and Roberts 2005), Jenny and I aimed to establish as much parity in our roles as possible, whilst acknowledging that I would hold clinical responsibility. By sharing the dynamic administration, attending joint supervision and incorporating a weekly reflection time, it was possible for the group to be held by both of us. In the same way that a family is ideally held by two parents, so it seemed that the group was a safer environment when supported by two therapists.

In 'parenting' the group, we tried to keep in mind the possibility of modelling a flexible, sensitive relationship. In the opening scene, Jenny was able to spend time directly responding to an individual mother–child dyad, tuning in to Mally and Nia's tapping music, and directly supporting their interaction. I could remain at the piano and bring their contributions into the musical whole, holding together the other elements that were happening in the room. There is a parallel to be drawn here with a parental model, where one adult may be focused on an individual child's needs whilst the other is concerned with the family as a whole: the bigger picture.

At times in our musical relationship, Jenny and I followed our partner's musical lead, or provided challenge in our musical material when the other therapist appeared to be stuck. There were moments when we supported each other in our attempts to take new steps, such as when Jenny decided to sing for the first time in the group, tackling her inhibitions in the same way we expected the mothers to do. As parents may move in and out of these flexible roles, supporting, challenging and leading each other, so Jenny and I attempted to model a way of relating that may have been difficult for the mother–child dyads to achieve with each other.

Working with two therapists also allows for the possibility of two different perspectives on the group. Although this could feel exposing or threatening, with adequate supervision and reflection time these differing perspectives offer a great strength. To best illustrate this, I want to use an example taken from a different clinical group, although one which follows the same model and also involves three mother–child dyads.

Sue and Ben

From the first sessions, Jenny and I notice that Sue, one of the mothers in the group, appears to relate very differently to us both. In the music time, Jenny often feels as if she isn't being given permission to interact with Sue's son, Ben. Sue avoids eye contact with Jenny and seems to cut across any interactions that begin to develop with her son. At such times, Jenny feels that her musical offerings are clumsy and as if she is 'getting it wrong'. Regularly in the sessions, Sue brings her son over to me at the piano and stands back as if to avoid getting in the way of this interaction. In the talking session, Sue asks me questions about Ben, wanting my opinion on interpretations of his behaviour. I feel as if I am being spoken to as the person in the group with authority, and that my thoughts are to be valued. After the session, Sue waits behind wishing to discuss issues relating to other aspects of school life.

In our reflection time, Jenny and I wonder about Sue's own parental models and consider how we may be experiencing something of her current family dynamics. Foulkes (1964) used the analogy of a jigsaw puzzle to illustrate this idea. He considered that a person in isolation is like a single piece of puzzle, which is meaningless unless it can be placed in the jigsaw. When an individual joins a therapy group, she tries to recreate the original jigsaw of her own family, shaping the other pieces (people) to fit. And so it is possible that the family becomes visible within the group.

Jenny and I decide not to comment directly on the way we experience Sue's relationship with us, but instead we hold on to our thinking and let it inform the way we respond. We attempt to keep in our heads being equal partners in the work, aware of the possibility of tension arising between us. In future talking sessions, when I am addressed directly about an opinion about Ben or a group administration issue, I ask Jenny how she feels about this, or refer to the group for their thoughts. In the music sessions, Jenny perseveres in her musical interactions with Ben and Sue, trying to find new ways of approaching whilst being sensitive about the quality time the two of them are spending together. Things gradually begin to shift. A month later, in our music session, Jenny approaches Ben with a shaker. He turns to face her and begins to bang the drum in an enthusiastic manner. Jenny plays along using his pulse and mood in her responses and they both laugh with pleasure. Sue watches the interaction, giving it space and looking pleased. She comments in the talking on how positive this moment is.

In this example, our different co-therapy experiences may have been very divisive. However, by acknowledging and exploring our feelings, a deeper understanding of the group members became possible. While the moments of tension between us were often the most difficult times in the group, they also proved to be the most useful, bringing about shifts and developments in the therapeutic process.

Managing the music and talking

I have stressed the importance of providing the mothers in the group with their own therapy space, a talking time to be heard as individuals, rather than simply mothers. As well as offering crucial support to the mothers, this model of music therapy containing a balance of music and talking gives the therapists two experiences of the family, explored through different media. The clinical examples used have often illustrated similar patterns of behaviour visible in both elements of the session. In the opening scene, for example, it was interesting to note how Ella and Iran were both able to make connections quickly with the other members of the group, Iran reaching out to another boy in the music session, and Ella offering friendly verbal overtures in the talking time. Having two distinct sections to the therapy provides the therapists with additional opportunities to learn about the group members and the way they relate to the world.

The clinical examples included in this chapter describe the music sessions as using free improvisations. In fact we always began the sessions with a familiar 'Hello' song, sung to the children individually; a song to acknowledge each child and mother pair; and in time we brought in one additional song to model the possibility of the boys acknowledging each other. After this rather more structured opening section, the session used free improvisation before closing with a 'Goodbye' song. In a previous piece of work, which also included multiple families, I used structured songs throughout the music session, feeling that such a large number of people in the room would be too chaotic to manage in free improvisation. I found the use of songs managed my own anxiety about tackling this large piece of work. This previous structure had its positive elements: it offered the parents a safe, familiar way of interacting and I could use the songs to focus attention on various ways of being together in the music. However, I became aware of the limitations. I began to feel constrained by the songs and found it hard to break free from them. I felt frustrated that I was leading the focus of the group rather than allowing it to develop at its own pace. In this recent model, by using an outside shell of a structure that moved between songs and improvisation, Jenny and I were able to move between modelling and allowing ourselves to be led by the group. It also seemed useful to find a line between routine and flexibility, which is particularly relevant for children with autism spectrum conditions, who can typically be rigid in their behaviours and find security in structure, but who have a need to manage flexibility in order to cope with an unpredictable world.

Conclusion

As Dickman and Gordon (1985) stated, 'it is not the child's disability that handicaps and disintegrates families; it is the way they react to it and to each other'. By offering music therapy to a mother, alongside her child, support is offered to these two members of a family. Through the pre-verbal musical medium they can revisit their playful interaction and explore relating to each other in new ways. The therapeutic support offered to the mother, the child and their relationship may in turn have an effect on the family as a whole. Perhaps they will begin to explore new possibilities in how they react to the child's disability and to each other. In some cases then, providing family music therapy may be the way to make the biggest difference to the life of a referred child.

For such families to come together in a group brings a further dimension to the therapy. Both mother and child can belong to a community. They have a place to celebrate their achievements and to explore their potentially difficult and painful emotions. The model discussed in this chapter aims to hold the resulting complexity of multiple families in one room by 'parenting' the group with a pair of therapists and by providing balance in the structure of the session: talking is balanced with playing and songs are balanced with improvisation.

Offering therapy to mothers seemed the obvious place to begin family work, particularly in a school setting where mothers are often the most available parent during the school day. The research examined supported this approach by suggesting that mothers managing autistic spectrum conditions are likely to experience the most stress. However, whilst writing this chapter I have become more aware of some of the difficulties which fathers may experience. Contact a Family (2006), for example, highlight a father's potential to feel excluded and uninformed as their partners frequently receive information in the family first. Daniel and Taylor (2001) stress that fathers are just as likely to exhibit attachment-promoting behaviours as mothers, and state that the more opportunity fathers have to be with their child the more these behaviours are shown. Offering music therapy to a group of fathers and their children, or perhaps a mixed group of parent–child dyads, could bring new perspectives and challenges to this therapeutic model and to the family of a child with autistic spectrum condition.

Chapter 5

'Who is the Therapy For?'
Involving a Parent or Carer in their Child's Music Therapy

Jasenka Horvat and Nicky O'Neill

Introduction

Working with children in music therapy inevitably implies working with their parents as well. Whether we see the parents in the waiting room, or have contact with them by telephone, letter or report in between sessions, a strong working alliance with the parents can have significant effect on the therapeutic process.

Within this chapter the focus in particular is on working with parents and carers together with their children in the music therapy room. Through the use of two cases, whose stories are woven together in this joint exploration, we aim to examine the possible reasons for actively including parents in sessions, the implications this might have on the clinical focus, and the changing roles within the therapeutic relationship. One of these cases included a parent in the room, while the other involved a grandmother.

At the time when we both trained (10 and 16 years ago, respectively) at the Nordoff-Robbins Music Therapy Centre, London, working with parents was an area not specifically covered within the curriculum, in theory or in practice. As we have developed our clinical practice, however, both within and outside the Nordoff-Robbins Centre, we found ourselves in constant contact with parents, before, during and after sessions. Issues about this often emerged in our clinical discussion groups in the Centre, prompting us, among other things, to engage in a collaborative research project that investigated parental involvement, including therapist–parent interactions in their children's music therapy (Procter 2005).

Thinking about the family context and its impact on the child opened us up to thinking more broadly about various modes of therapeutic intervention which might be most beneficial to the child, including actively involving parents in the sessions. One of the first questions that emerged for us was how to decide when to include the parent in the music therapy room.

Decision to include parents in the therapy room

Anna

(Therapist: Jasenka Horvat)

It is early 2001 and I am sitting with the Head of Clinical Services at the Nordoff-Robbins Centre, reading Anna's medical history and consultation report, and discussing her case.

Anna lost her hearing completely as a result of the meningitis that she contracted when she was just over one year old, and which almost killed her. From a very alert and forward child she became withdrawn, silent and insecure, with all the aspects of her development suddenly arrested. She could not walk, stopped speaking and using her voice, and even her hair stopped growing.

Anna's parents, both deeply traumatised by the tragic events surrounding Anna's illness, were particularly devastated by her hearing loss. Both of them, being professional musicians, regarded music not as 'an optional extra', but a vitally important and essential aspect of life. The thought that their daughter would be deprived of it was utterly disheartening for them.

Anna's grandmother, Lisa, played a significant role in taking care of not just Anna, but the whole family in those difficult times. For her, the fact that Anna survived was nothing short of a miracle, and she celebrated every little step that Anna was making in her recovery. She brought Anna to music therapy in the hope that it might somehow assist her rehabilitation, giving her an opportunity to develop listening skills once she was fitted with the cochlear implant.[1] She was just 20 months old at the time.

Both the Head of Clinical Services and I feel that because of Anna's young age, traumatic experiences and safety (Anna was to start her sessions just a week after her cochlear implant operation) it would be good to have

---

1   A cochlear implant is a special hearing aid device which can be implanted directly into the cochlear part of the ear in cases of profound hearing loss. It consists of a small processor that transforms sound waves into electrical impulses, which are then directly transmitted to the brain. As it is primarily designed to pick up speech frequencies, the quality of music reception through it is questionable.

someone close and familiar with her in the therapy room. For practical reasons, it seemed that her grandmother rather than Anna's parents would take that role.

At the same time, I feel that I am stepping into the big unknown. I have never worked with a child's family member in the room before. How is it going to work? Will I feel intimidated or judged? Will I be able to engage freely with the child while being closely observed all the time? Ultimately, am I good enough, confident in my role as a music therapist? And, what is my role going to be in this context?

At the Nordoff-Robbins Centre the initial recommendation as to whether or not to include a parent in the therapy room is often made during the consultation session, as in Anna's case. Some of the elements that might be considered are the child's age, diagnosis, difficulties in relating to the parent, their level of anxiety, the family context and reasons for referral. Sometimes, however, as in the next case, it is not until the first session that the need to include the parent in the room becomes apparent.

Pedro
(Therapist: Nicky O'Neill)

Pedro has been referred to the Nordoff-Robbins Centre by his health visitor. He is five years old, with severe learning and communication difficulties, and challenging behaviour, including self-harming and aggression towards others. The recommendation from the consultation session is that Pedro is seen alone by an experienced therapist in order to work on his difficulties as well as his ability to be more independent from his mother. His family context was taken into consideration, whereby his mother, as the main carer, struggled to carve any space for herself owing to his constant emotional and physical demands.

When I collect Pedro for his first session from the reception area in the Nordoff-Robbins Centre I suggest saying 'goodbye' to his mother, Lola, and coming with me into the therapy room on his own. Pedro immediately starts kicking, screaming and attacking his mother. It is clear that Lola finds this behaviour difficult to manage and, after chastising him verbally, gives in to his demands for her to accompany him into the therapy room.

I decide not to intervene, but rather to observe and respond to what is happening between Lola and Pedro. I notice how Lola's response to Pedro's outbursts not only does not contain him, but further exacerbates his challenging behaviour. Before we know it, all three of us are in the therapy room, not knowing what's going to happen.

Here, rather than making a premeditated decision to invite the parent to join the child in the therapy room, the therapist had to assess the presenting situation promptly and make a decision on the spot.

It is only as the therapeutic process evolves, however, and the focus of the therapy becomes apparent, that we can make a more informed decision about how to involve the parent. Through observing the nature of the parent–child relationship, as presented through their interactions in the therapy room, it becomes possible to identify the child and parent's needs and what format of therapeutic intervention would be most beneficial: to have the parent in the therapy room or not, or whether, for example, the parent might need additional support for themselves separately from the child's therapy.

Sometimes the initial recommendation from the consultation session about the nature of parents' involvement is confirmed; at other times it is necessary to make changes.

Changing focus, changing roles

Pedro

Once in the room their negative spiral continues, with Lola telling Pedro to 'go and play the instruments with Nicky!' Pedro responds with aggression towards Lola, as well as careering in a disorganised and unpredictable way around the room. He hits the drum and cymbal briefly with real force, before seemingly becoming overwhelmed by the strength of his expression: he screams, throws the beaters and pushes over the instruments.

I find myself struggling to maintain safe physical boundaries and establish musical connection at the same time. In the brief moments of Pedro's musical engagement, he is beating on the drum and cymbal in short, loud and forceful outbursts, which, after a dramatic accelerando, culminate in him pushing the instruments over. He grimaces as he plays, often looking towards me, seemingly aware of my attempts to match his playing exactly on the piano, in rhythm, timbre and emotional content. After pushing the instruments over, he runs to his mother continuing with physical aggression towards her. He is no longer able to listen to me, as they become locked in a physical struggle.

In an attempt to facilitate a more contained, and, for Pedro, more manageable musical expression, in subsequent sessions I offered more structured activities based on familiar nursery rhymes. Similarly, this seemed to be able to engage him only for brief moments, again resulting inevitably in outbursts of aggression towards Lola.

Invariably, they would leave the session and the Centre amidst a flurry of physical aggression and at full volume.

I found myself powerfully affected by the dynamics in the room, seemingly being pulled into a whirlpool of reacting to the situation rather than being able to think more objectively. I was wondering whether this was how Lola experienced herself in relation to Pedro, not being able to separate physically or mentally from him, confused and unconfident in her parenting role, as I was, at the time, in my therapist's role. It was significant that it was not possible for us to find either the time or a way to talk or think together about the therapy process, after or in between sessions. I felt strongly that I wanted a separate space to think about these issues and needed support from my supervisor in order to, in turn, be able to offer support to Lola in developing a more confident parenting role.

It became apparent from analysing the sessions with my supervisor that, in order to work on Pedro's difficulties as they presented in the room, it was necessary to address the patterns of behaviour embedded within Pedro and Lola's relationship. This meant a shift in the focus of the therapy, as I perceived it, from focusing on building a musical relationship with Pedro to focusing on, as Oldfield and Bunce (2001, p.27) describe it, 'nurturing and encouraging a positive relationship between the mother and the child.'

Another thing that emerged in the supervision was the need to enable Lola to experience different ways of being with her child and to offer her an opportunity to increase the range of skills in relating to and interacting with him. Rather than discussing this with her, it seemed that, on the basis of our previous interactions, the most effective approach would be to demonstrate this to Lola practically.

I propose the altered focus of the sessions to Lola in a casual manner as we walk down the corridor to the room, suggesting that 'In order to help Pedro, let's all make music together today, with you joining in as well.' Lola seems intrigued and playfully smiles back in agreement.

I have changed the layout of the room, placing a floor mat and three little chairs in a circle. We start with me singing a 'Hello' song, playfully offering the tambourine to each person to play in turn on the beat. Lola immediately joins in with singing and the instrumental playing in a very natural and easy way. She seems to enjoy herself in this new musical role. Pedro's face reveals surprise and wonderment at his mother's enthusiastic participation, and he engages with matching eagerness. This continues for the rest of the session where I lead us through differently structured musical activities based on clearly defined turn-taking, which allow balancing between initiating and following each other's musical ideas.

They leave smiling and apparently enjoying each other, with Lola commenting, 'That was fun, Pedro!'

When I was thinking before the session how best to facilitate this altered clinical focus, I thought carefully about the layout of the room and the musical structure of the session. It seemed to me that putting three chairs in a circle would immediately suggest not only including Lola in our joint music-making in a more equal way, but also recognising her vital role within their difficult relationship.

With their relationship in focus my role now was to model, facilitate and enable Lola and Pedro to experience different ways of relating and interacting with each other through making music together. This role, however, was not new for me, as I suddenly realised that the changed clinical focus resulted in altering the lens through which I perceived this therapy; from starting with individual therapy with the child, I was now approaching it more as group music therapy. My role shifted from leader and modeller to facilitator, monitor, occasional leader and receptive follower, aiming to stand back wherever possible, allowing Lola's budding initiative to flourish. In analysing what I did in the sessions I was reminded of Pavlicevic's (2003, pp.89–90) descriptions of tasks that music therapists might adopt within group music therapy context. While monitoring what was happening in the room, both musically and relationally, I was trying to enable both Pedro's and Lola's individual and joined creativity to emerge, fostering their musical and personal relationship. My introducing of playful turn-taking structures, for example, allowed each of their musical personalities to emerge by giving each person an individual voice and time in which to be heard and listened to. This provided both Lola and Pedro with an opportunity to hear and experience each other as separate individuals and to learn how to respond more sensitively and to attune to each other. Lola seemed relieved with her more defined role, which not only elevated her from her observer/policing role but also gave her the opportunity to participate musically.

In order to empower Lola in her parenting role, I felt it was important for her not to experience me as an 'expert' but rather as a facilitator, whose musical and therapeutic interventions allowed their conflict, as well as new patterns of relating and interacting with one another, to be 'sounded' and heard.

Sometimes it was necessary for me to take a more active lead by providing musical activities and structures which were manageable for both Pedro and Lola (introducing, for example, short musical activities and moving on to the next one before Pedro lost focus and regressed into an unregulated state of overexcitement and aggression). At other times I was following, acutely alert to and seizing every moment when Lola or Pedro might take the initiative. As the sessions progressed, Lola gradually began to initiate more by bringing in the songs and musical material that were familiar to her and Pedro. This demonstrated Lola's growing confidence not only in her musical role in the sessions but also in her parental role where she could allow herself to relax and be more playful with Pedro, rather than needing to assert her role through disciplining and chastising him all the time. She was also increasingly sensitive in her responses to Pedro and able to balance between initiating and following his musical ideas, thus giving him the opportunity to take part and have influence over our musical interaction in ways that were very different to previously.

Above all, my listening to both of them with 'focus, commitment, openness and attentiveness' (Pavlicevic 2003, p.90), and holding the feelings of Pedro and Lola in a space which was 'safe' for them to express and begin to work through some of the gamut of their emotions, not only enabled the therapy process but gave Lola a model of behaviour for relating to her child.

Whereas for Pedro the focus of the therapy was on offering different ways for this mother and child to relate to each other, for Anna, the direction of the work was more concerned with addressing her developmental and emotional needs while working on developing her relationship with music. The strong and positive emotional bond between her and her grandmother, Lisa, played a crucial role. Throughout the three and a half years of her therapy Lisa accompanied Anna in her music therapy journey with sensitivity, acutely attuned and attentive to the therapist's clinical direction, as well as to Anna's physical and emotional needs and responses.

Anna

It is one of our early sessions and Lisa comes into the room holding a distressed Anna in her arms. Anna is curled up and nuzzling into Lisa's collar, sucking the material for comfort. I suggest sitting together by the piano, with me playing for Anna. The music I play gently picks up Lisa's rocking movement, while reflecting Anna's emotional state by following the rhythmic and melodic contours of her quiet sobbing. Gradually, Anna calms down and Lisa gently uncurls her from her lap and turns her toward the keyboard, placing her hands on the piano. Anna watches my fingers intently and then starts to play herself.

★ ★ ★

Anna is just over two years old now and is sitting on Lisa's lap, listening and watching intently while I am singing a familiar nursery rhyme to her, trying to elicit her vocal responses. I carefully pitch my voice within a range, volume and in a tempo that I sense would be manageable for Anna to join in, with spaces which I leave for her. Lisa's attentive and focused listening and presence support my musical intervention and these result in Anna finding the confidence to start using her voice.

★ ★ ★

Anna is now three years old and has discovered her dancing body. It is the beginning of the session and she is poised for her usual 'opening dancing sequence'. She turns to me expectantly waiting for me to start playing, holding her arms up as a signal for Lisa to lift her. I accompany this with ascending arpeggios in a lilting three-four rhythm, followed by descending ones on her way back down. This is repeated several times before Anna moves on to the next part of her choreography. Whilst she is experimenting with different movements, I support and enhance this from the piano. Lisa is joining Anna by mirroring her balletic attempts and further defining them.

Through this combined interplay with each of us initiating and following, Anna obviously enjoys the experience of co-creativity in which she is the focal part. Her dancing becomes more confident and daring. When at one point she trips and falls, Lisa falls too, while I accompany it musically, thereby turning this into a creative feature of the dance. Anna is obviously encouraged with this unreserved acceptance of her whole self and immediately continues dancing with renewed confidence.

★ ★ ★

Anna is now four and her sessions are filled with dramatic musical stories that she brings to life through freely using musical instruments, her speaking and singing voice and dancing. Lisa is now an equal playmate who is taking on different imaginary roles as instructed by Anna. I accompany, illustrate, follow or initiate dramatic developments in the story. Lisa and I are now stretched to follow Anna's creative direction, with her now confidently in the leading role, while creating her musical 'performances'.

★ ★ ★

It is our final session. Anna is almost five and we are improvising on two pianos, while Lisa is quietly sitting and listening. Our playing is very expressive and dramatic, encapsulating all the drama that was previously expressed through her musical stories. She leads us in the final cadence which she finishes confidently with a single note in the low register. After a brief silence she turns towards Lisa with a smile of satisfying accomplishment and pleasure. Lisa smiles back, applauding and celebrating Anna's achievement.

★ ★ ★

When looking back over the years with Anna, it seems strange to recall the anxieties that I felt at the beginning of the work. I was unsure how I might work with Lisa in the room, and not clear what her role might be. As our relationships developed, however, including Anna's emerging relationship with the music, it becomes clear that Lisa's sensitive and responsive manner added much to the work. The role of co-therapist, which emerged for her, proved crucial in the work, in particular in:

- building up Anna's self-confidence in experimenting with sounds, both instrumentally and vocally
- helping her to make sense of the sounds (through a shared emotional experience)
- encouraging her self-expression
- supporting the development of her creative play
- providing reassurance and emotional support.

This brings to mind Nordoff and Robbins's description of co-therapy:

When therapy is undertaken by a team it is essential that the abilities and efforts of both therapists combine closely and freely to attain these aims. This requires that the relationship between the team members is one of partners sharing in the creativeness, the events and the responsibilities of the therapy. The role of the pianist is to engage the child musically in a developmentally effective way, while the role of the assistant is to support the pianist's work, to supplement it resourcefully in whatever way the situation calls for. (Nordoff and Robbins 1977, pp.91–92)

More than that, though, Lisa and Anna brought into the room the existing strength and closeness of their relationship. This itself introduced a new dimension to the work, their intimately attuned relationship being available to us all as a therapeutic tool. I felt increasingly able to make use of this tool and also privileged to be part of it.

Conclusion

As music therapy practitioners we have increasingly encountered clinical situations where parents take an active role as participant in the therapy room with their child. The reasons might vary from parents providing physical or emotional support for the child, to those where difficulties in the child–parent relationship become the main focus of the therapy.

In Anna's case the whole therapy process was built around and enabled by her pre-existing, positive relationship and strong emotional bond with her grandmother. When working on developing Anna's ability to receive, respond and express herself through music, the therapist made use of this relationship thus enabling Anna to achieve the desired clinical goals.

In Pedro's case, by contrast, his difficult and troubled relationship with his mother became the main focus of the therapy. Here, the therapist's thinking and approach had to expand from a child-centred to a more family-centred intervention – the main aims being concerned with the improved and increased interactions between parent and child.

Although the reasons for including the parents or carers in the therapy room in the above two cases were very different, there were also many similarities. Both of these carers were an integral part of the therapy, both were equally needed by their child and both, in their different roles, were ready to engage actively in their child's therapy. Each was encouraged to draw on their own individual and innate musicianship. For Lola, experiencing herself being confident and playful in her musical role with her son, and exploring different ways of musical interaction, enhanced the development of her parenting skills outside the room. For Lisa, sharing her own creative expression and enjoyment freely with her grandchild, and witnessing this, enabled Anna, in turn, to explore with more confidence the possibilities of her own musical expressions.

Building a strong working alliance and a trusting relationship with the carers is crucial whether they are in or out of the room. Within this context we need to take the responsibility to extend our therapeutic role beyond the boundaries of the therapy room if we are to offer the most effective intervention.

We need to think carefully about the aims, methods and clinical applications of our work with parents as well as the nature of the engagement that we offer. There are various elements and contexts that need to be considered when deciding whether or how to include parents in the therapy room. What is most important for us as therapists, however, is the need to be constantly attentive to the changing clinical demands throughout the therapeutic process and to be able to offer and move flexibly between different modalities of therapeutic intervention.

Our work at the Nordoff-Robbins Centre with parents actively involved in their children's sessions began from a more accidental basis. This prompted us and our colleagues to look at and research this particular clinical area more closely. As a result, we have included some important changes to the structure of our clinical practice:

- working with parents in the room is now regarded as one of the important options to be considered in the consultation session

- the importance of building a strong working alliance with parents, in or out of the therapy room, is now recognised

- more time is allocated within the timetable for meeting with parents before and after sessions

- the complexity and possible challenges when working with parents are recognised, and the extra support is provided for therapists through the clinical management structure as well as peer supervision

- we are actively working on including this clinical area within the Nordoff–Robbins training course as well as our own continuing professional development.

Working with parents in the room initially felt like something new and quite alien to our working within the Nordoff-Robbins tradition. However, one of the most salient points of this tradition is to follow the client's needs, and by doing exactly that we were naturally responding by expanding and adapting the nature of our involvement with the parents. In our work, as described above, we drew on some aspects of therapy work which stemmed from working as co-therapists and in a group context. Our main focus on facilitating clients to develop as deep and meaningful a relationship to music as possible remained the same. We discovered in the process that by engaging with this particular clinical area we have enriched and expanded both our practice and theoretical framework.

Coda for Anna

Anna is today very comfortably and confidently settled in her mainstream school; she is at the top of the class in reading and she enjoys her ballet classes and her piano lessons. She also spends a long time just freely improvising on the piano, and likes Lisa to sit beside her so she can tell her what her 'compositions' are about. These are often stories not unlike those she made in her sessions, but this time not acted out but internalised and expressed through her playing. When Lisa once asked her what was she hearing while she was playing, she replied, 'It's not what I hear, it's what I see!' In her own way, Anna has developed an ability not only to receive and make a sense of musical sounds, but also to use them creatively and meaningfully for her spontaneous self-expression.

Coda for Pedro

After four months of joint therapy with Pedro and Lola, they were now ready for more independence. When I met them in the reception area for the first session back after the Christmas holidays, Lola announced that Pedro was ready now to come with me into the therapy room without her. Unlike the first session, when she was trying to make him come to the session by himself, this confident announcement came from a very different place. It seemed as if she was voicing what we all intuitively felt was needed as the next step in his therapy, focusing on his needs independently from her. After a little encouragement from both of us, Pedro willingly went into the therapy room with just me.

Pedro remains a child with significant difficulties with his communication and learning skills, as well as his ability to regulate his behaviour. This is the focus of his ongoing therapy. As Lola has experienced and witnessed the effect that different ways of her relating to Pedro have on his behaviour and their relationship, she is now more able to perceive them objectively and therefore differentiate between his strengths and needs and their relationship difficulties. She is increasingly attuned to Pedro and able to respond appropriately, recognising and appreciating his whole personality.

Chapter 6

Music Therapy with Traumatised Children and their Families in Mainstream Primary Schools
A Case Study with a Six-Year-Old Girl and her Mother

Sarah Howden

This chapter explores the progression from one-to-one music therapy sessions with children in their mainstream primary school, to family music therapy, where their parents arc invited to attend the sessions with them. A case study will illustrate some of the factors to be considered when taking the therapy in this new direction and will demonstrate how such a transition can work.

I have worked in three mainstream primary schools in north London over the past six years, offering one-to-one, group and family music therapy. The schools are in areas of socio-economic deprivation and the majority of the children I see have witnessed or been the victim of some highly traumatic event involving violence.

Before looking at how one-to-one sessions progress to family sessions, it is necessary to consider how music therapy is viewed in the mainstream schools where I work. When I started, it seemed that the only therapeutic support available to families locally was through National Health Service (NHS) organisations. It transpired that, among parents, there was a fear of labelling attached to referrals to see a psychotherapist or clinical psychologist, with some refusing to take their children to appointments. When setting up my practice, I felt it was essential to communicate clearly and succinctly what music therapy involved before any fantasies developed about the term 'therapy'. I invited teachers, parents and professionals from external agencies to meet me and visit the music therapy room, a bright, child-friendly space. Their response was extremely positive, with many commenting that they wished they had the opportunity to play the huge variety of instruments. Music has long played a large part in the primary school child's life, from singing hymns in assembly to using nursery rhymes when learning the alphabet. Some parents understandably fixated on the word 'music', imagining that I would play soothing, relaxing pieces to their child. I clarified the role music plays in sessions, detailing its qualities as a vehicle for free self-expression and demonstrating how the music created could indeed be relaxing and soothing, but equally it could be loud, chaotic and even uncomfortable. I also explained the focus on shared improvisation and interaction through which therapeutic work can take place. It was crucial to distinguish between music therapy and music education, and I found that parents and professionals embraced the concept of using music as a therapeutic tool when working with young, vulnerable children, in terms of it helping them to feel safe enough to communicate something of their traumatic experience.

Initially, referrals were made solely through the schools' special educational needs co-ordinators, but this has now expanded to include taking referrals from head teachers, class teachers and educational psychologists. Occasionally, a parent requests a meeting with me before granting permission for their child's music therapy, questioning why their child needs 'therapy', concerned that they will be labelled as having special needs and, at times, worried about what their child might share verbally about their 'business indoors'. While addressing their concerns I focus on their child's behaviour in school and stress how time away from class for self-expression through music might be beneficial. I also explain the confidentiality of the sessions and how I will report on a child's music therapy process in multi-disciplinary reviews and parent meetings, but I cannot disclose exactly what their child shares in terms of words or actions. No parent has refused permission for music therapy to date.

For parents and some professionals, the idea of a child receiving therapeutic support in the consistent, familiar surroundings of their primary school has often seemed preferable to such care in other settings. The safety of the child's school environment has also touched those parents whom I have invited to join sessions, in particular those who were unwilling or afraid to engage as a family with support in the past.

Pupils themselves generally view music therapy as something fun and exciting, if not a little mysterious. I'm usually referred to as 'Sarah, the music lady', who gives special music lessons. This idea has been shaped by the children I work with, who develop a good understanding of music therapy, but prefer to tell their peers that they simply do music and that it is private. As a result, I have never observed any negative stigma attached to attending music therapy among pupils.

After a period of one-to-one music therapy with a child, I sometimes find that it is beneficial to include a parent in sessions, thus taking the therapy in a new direction, that of family music therapy. This initially came about when I felt that some children's difficulties lay within family relationships and that I was only reaching part of their story in our one-to-one sessions. Increasingly, I believed that involving members of the child's family in the music therapy process would allow me to focus on these difficulties directly and support them more effectively. Having discussed my ideas with the schools' special educational needs co-ordinators, I was given permission to take the therapy in this new direction, inviting families into the school if I felt it was the right step. I took this chance and found the work to be very successful.

It is important to note that the idea for such a transition evolves from within the therapeutic process and many factors require careful consideration before such a decision is made. In my experience to date, it has always been one parent who attends the sessions, owing to being a one-parent family or because the second parent has work commitments or younger siblings to look after. There have been some instances when I have worked with a parent and all of their children together in sessions, not just the child I saw originally. The following case study illustrates how the move from one-to-one music therapy with a child to family sessions can work.

Susie

Susie, a six-year-old Portuguese girl, was referred to me because of her aggression in class. She would lash out viciously at other children in a bid to get her own way and she had the air of a teenager, confidently arguing with teachers and showing no remorse for her actions. During my preliminary observations, I noted that she was disliked by children and adults alike, and she reminded me of 'Veruca Salt' in Roald Dahl's *Charlie and the Chocolate Factory*, expecting her impulsive whims be met immediately. Susie found it impossible to share anything with her peers and she was on the school's Special Educational Needs Register for challenging behaviour.

Susie lived alone with her mother, Mrs S, aged 41, who was a part-time nurse caring for the elderly. Susie's father had been brutally murdered two and a half years earlier, just before her fourth birthday. A youth had entered the family's chip shop, demanding money, but Mr S had squared up to him, brandishing a hammer he kept under the cash desk for protection. The burglar's unnoticed accomplice grabbed the hammer from behind, then beat Mr S's head repeatedly, killing him almost instantly. Witnesses led to the capture of the killers, who were subsequently sent to prison.

This was not the only traumatic event in Susie's young life. She was born with a dislocated hip, which went undiagnosed until she was over a year old. She had since undergone numerous operations both to correct this and to improve the appearance of extensive scarring.

The first year

Susie approached her initial sessions with great confidence, readily engaging in improvisation and shouting instructions to me over our playing. If I asked her to share a structured musical activity, she would, but she turned everything into a competition. Given the choice, Susie opted not to share, preferring to be the performer and monopolising the session as she demonstrated how well she could play, smiling throughout. Her music had a desperate quality to it since she played everything rapidly, often standing on her tiptoes with the effort. She also played without pulse, lending a chaotic feel to her performance. When she finished, she would smile and make a smug comment of self-congratulation, then instantly move on to play something else, without waiting for me to say a word.

In our first session, Susie told me that she lived with her mummy and that her daddy was an angel in heaven with God. Without any show of emotion, she explained how her father had been killed by some 'bad men', her gestures communicating that she knew every detail of the attack. Her bright facial expression noticeably contrasted with the subject matter of her story. I said simply, 'Susie, that is very sad about your daddy.' Smiling, she replied, 'He is still with me every day, looking down at me doing things.' As she spoke, I gained an impression that Susie was simply reciting what she herself had been told, possibly by her mother.

Susie also talked about her numerous hip operations. She explained that she didn't like people looking at her scars so she wore tracksuit bottoms in PE. This caused her to stand out from her classmates who did PE in their vests and pants. She admitted that if anyone looked at her as she changed, she went and hit them.

Susie was clearly a very verbal child. When talking openly about her experiences, I was struck by how she consistently presented as 'smiley' and happy, and I sensed that she was 'emotionally dissociated'. Sutton (2004) describes 'dissociation' as a response which allows the child to absent themself psychologically following repeated exposure to significant trauma. This may later become a conditioned response to any distressing experience. I wondered if this was the case for Susie.

Susie continued to show no range in her music, always playing instruments as fast as she could. In our sixth session, I encouraged her to share the piano with me and engage in improvised songs. We took turns to sing phrases, Susie making up the story, playing rapid chords at the treble end of the piano. Through song I reflected her ideas, pulling the detail together, whilst instilling drama into her story through my piano accompaniment. I often use improvised song stories in my work, encouraging children to develop a tale in their own direction. Oldfield (2000) describes this technique, explaining that, through improvised stories, children may show emotions that have not come to the fore before and they may indirectly share concerns that shed light on trauma they may have experienced.

Susie developed long tales connected to her father's death, and through these I had a sense of her family being a part of our sessions. This was particularly so for her father, who in his absence from her life was actually very present. Her musical stories centred on a little girl gathering all of her relatives, including her mum, to the family's shop, where she would strangle them, keeping their money and the shop for herself. She sang about how 'bad' and 'horrid' the little girl was.

In reality, Susie herself was often called a 'bad girl' by her peers and her teacher, and this led her to identify with the 'bad men' who had killed her father. She seemed to fantasise that she was no better than them and therefore capable of doing what they had done.

During this time, I made one simple link for Susie; that the way the little girl killed her family in their shop reminded me of her daddy being killed in his family's shop. Susie agreed that it was like this. Showing appropriate emotion for the first time, she then spoke angrily about hating the 'bad men' who did this to her daddy. I encouraged her to sing about this, injecting emotion into her ideas using crashing dissonant chords. De Backer (1993, p.36) describes this accompaniment by the music therapist as 'stretching a skin over the patient's experience', the music binding and shaping the client's expression. Explaining the concept of containment in music therapy, De Backer and Van Camp (1999, p.19) write: 'Music therapy provides the possibility of expressing alarming and unbearable experiences by improvising on musical instruments...the music therapist does not remain passive through all this but tries to accompany and shape the musical outburst...the patient no longer feels that these confused feelings and the fact of not being understood are unbearable.' The therapist accepts the client's ideas without becoming alarmed, thus leading them to feel 'contained'. Susie mirrored my playing and I hoped that through her music she would truly start to connect with her anger. The booming chords acted as a container through which she could safely vent her immediate feelings about her father's death. Susie spent several sessions pouring out her thoughts through song, sharing her wish that she could see her father's killers so that she could kill them herself.

As we played what Susie now termed 'angry music', I accepted her ideas without judgement, which led her to let go and express herself increasingly freely. Together, we gradually made more connections verbally between the music and her experiences and feelings.

Susie's improvised story about the little girl developed. She sang of her heroine buying all the toys that she wanted. Through song, I asked what happened next and Susie sang of the girl feeling bored and lonely and starting to miss her family. Our loud, dissonant chords gave way to melancholic, beautiful melodies and we sang duets, our voices overlapping as our vocal passages ascended higher and higher. Susie's voice became softer and increasingly strained, eventually taking on a whimpering quality. Through this musical expression I sensed Susie letting her guard down, the domineering character giving way to a vulnerable little girl. Particularly striking was the way she mingled her voice with mine, actively seeking moments of sustained unison without competition.

Susie sang of the little girl's family coming alive again through magic and how they forgave the girl for her 'badness'. This led us to talk about giving people fresh chances to change their ways. Susie ended one particular session by clearly saying that she would never forgive the 'bad men' who killed her father. Although this was perfectly understandable, I considered that Susie perhaps felt she could not forgive herself for her 'bad' thoughts.

As Susie expressed herself freely and healthily through music in our sessions, I worked closely with her class teacher, planning strategies to support Susie in class. Susie had clear patterns of behaviour and her class teacher began to recognise these and situations when Susie might lash out, preempting them with a look or calm word, giving Susie pause for thought, preventing her from following her impulse through. A combination of music therapy and carefully devised support from her class teacher led Susie's behaviour in school to settle dramatically. I felt she was no longer over-whelmed by her complex fantasies and her self-perception was changing. With permission to express herself freely through the safety of musical activities, she no longer relied on violence towards her peers for release.

The second year

In our second year of music therapy, Susie developed a repeated imaginative play where I was the neighbour trying to sleep and she was the mother of a noisy child (a teddy bear) who drummed loudly all night, keeping me awake. Throughout the weeks of this play, I acted in various ways, sometimes com-plaining politely or with anger or pretending to weep because I was so tired. Susie consistently told me in an innocent voice that it was not her child making the noise. On one occasion I pretended to call the police. Susie immediately stopped the game, saying, 'Wait! Don't do that. Pretend the policeman is my daddy so he won't be cross with me drumming.' I noted that until now Susie had been acting the role of the mother, but she now related the play to herself as the noisy child. It was interesting that she didn't feel a parent would be cross with her for upsetting the neighbours with her noise. When I acted buying earplugs and slept through her drumming, she screamed and thrashed the cymbal, then stopped the game and said, 'Pretend you didn't buy earplugs.' If I challenged her and said, 'Hang on, can't we share the game?' or 'What happens if I want to play it this way?' she would instantly give in and let me play my way.

After several sessions playing out this scenario, I wondered aloud whether Susie was always the baddie because she thought she was a bad person. She replied, 'I have bad thoughts about the men who killed my daddy. I think about him every day and am happy on the outside, but I'm sad and think bad things on the inside.' I explained that she was not bad for feeling angry with the men or sometimes wishing she could hurt them back. I said that her daddy should not have been killed and that some days she might feel angry, some days she might feel sad and some days she might feel happy, remembering him. It was important to accept Susie's thoughts as natural. The expression, 'you're only human' comes to mind, as it is human nature to feel a range of emotions after a traumatic experience. These emotions will tend to find an outlet, overwhelming the individual, and leading to their release. Difficulty may arise when an emotional reaction is tightly controlled or repressed because it is considered unhealthy or is frowned upon, for example, crying. It is well documented how unexpressed grief or emotion after a traumatic event can lead to emotional and physical difficulties later on. I felt that Susie's story was tragic and I spoke of some of the emotions that I imagined she might have about her father's death, communicating that it would be natural for her to feel them and think of him, as she had said, every day.

Returning to the 'neighbour game' after this conversation, I suggested that we swap roles. Susie readily became the neighbour trying to sleep and I was the mother with the noisy child (the teddy bear). Susie complained furiously when my child's drumming woke her in the night. I apologised, then called my child to me, explaining how unkind they had been. I acted my child apologising then playing soothing music to help the neighbour sleep. From then on Susie steered our imaginative play in a new direction. We were kind, friendly neighbours with several children (teddy bears) who played together. Through musical drama, Susie was able to try on the role of different characters, exploring various ways of relating to others.

Following a very settled period, I was surprised when Susie was suspended from school for one week during the spring term of our second year. It transpired that another girl had glanced at the scars on her hip as they changed for PE, so Susie had viciously scratched her face, causing the other child permanent scarring.

In our next session, Susie played loud, uncontrolled music, explaining that she felt angry. It was a very positive step that she could now express emotion intentionally and healthily through music. She eventually explained that she had overheard her mum speaking on the telephone, saying that Susie's doctor did not notice that her leg was in the wrong place when she was born and if he had, she could have worn double nappies and been fine without all the operations and scars. The timing of this phone call coincided with Susie's attack on her classmate and subsequent suspension from school. I helped her to connect the two incidents; however, she expressed no remorse for hurting the other girl.

Meeting mum

Soon after this, the school's special educational needs co-ordinator met Susie and her mother, Mrs S, to discuss Susie's progress in school. The co-ordinator reported that whilst they were very affectionate towards one another, Susie constantly interrupted her mother, often correcting something she'd said in a scornful voice. Mrs S did not reprimand her daughter for her rude interruptions. When they left, Susie ordered her mother to carry her bag, which she did.

Following this report, I met Susie's mother, who seemed to be very depressed. She explained that she had no control over Susie, who saw herself as an equal and expected to have everything mum herself had. Mrs S said she just didn't have the energy to battle with her daughter, who in any case, deserved to be put first and given what she wanted, considering everything she'd been through. She explained that Susie had been much longed for and was conceived through IVF, and she wept as she shared a memory of her husband falling asleep in the garden with Susie as an infant in his arms.

Their relationship was clearly unbalanced in terms of who was playing the more dominant role. Mrs S gave everything to her child and this pattern of behaviour may have developed when her husband died or when Susie had her operations and Mrs S wanted to make things better for her. It could have been the result of waiting so long to have a baby in the first place.

Transition to family music therapy

As previously reported, Susie and her mother had an affectionate, loving relationship, but it was adversely affected by complex feelings they carried for one another, including guilt, blame and anger. I started to consider how working with Susie and her mother together in music therapy could allow me to observe and address dysfunctional patterns in their relationship. My one-to-one sessions with Susie were going very well, but I felt we could only go so far without her mother's input.

Many of the parents I meet are struggling with their own depression, taking little time to look after themselves as they focus on supporting their child in the aftermath of a traumatic experience. In family work, I consider the child to be my primary focus or primary client, so I have to weigh up how much I am going to work with the parent's depression whilst addressing their relationship with their child. It is important to keep the focus on the child in any preliminary conversations with the parent, whilst not disregarding their needs. Sometimes it is enough simply to mention that the parent seems depressed. In a way this gives them permission to recognise it themselves and I can then advise them of further support in the area.

Although parents readily accept their child having music therapy, it can be a different story when they consider the idea of attending something with the word 'therapy' in the title themself. Keeping the focus on the child can help to put them at ease.

When deciding to invite a parent to join sessions, we must recognise that a change in dynamics is inevitable. We also need to consider who to approach with the idea first, and this changes from family to family. In Susie's case, I wondered if she would reject the idea, wishing to keep her special music therapy time to herself, and how it might affect the balance of our relationship if I allowed her to control this decision. On the other hand, if Susie liked the idea, but her mum refused to come, would she take this as a personal rejection?

In this particular case, I put the idea to Mrs S first, explaining my belief that music therapy could help her in coping with Susie. I recognised that Mrs S might feel uncomfortable coming into school, where she might be seen by another parent, child or member of staff, so I assured her that the session would be held at a time when the school's corridors and grounds were quiet. I explained that I had not yet mentioned the idea to Susie and it was possible that she might want to keep the sessions and all the instruments to herself. Mrs S understood and said she would not mention our conversation to Susie until I had spoken to her. Mrs S was keen to come, desperate for any help in dealing with Susie. When I put the idea to Susie, she was very excited at the prospect of her mum joining her special music time.

Susie and I had four more one-to-one sessions, ending this chapter of our work and preparing for Mrs S to join us. I encouraged Susie to think about how the sessions would work with her mum and she suggested various musical games. Her plan to move away from story-telling and imaginative play did not seem strange, since the new ingredient of a parent changes the sessions and children often respond to this, even before we begin.

Family music therapy sessions

Before the first family session, I meet the parent to explain a little of my approach and how we can play music in any way we please, preempting that they might understandably say, for example, 'Don't play so loud' to their child when we get started. I also say that there will be a greeting song, then their child will share a bit about what we do. I keep this conversation brief, wishing the child to be involved in setting up our group sessions.

It is important in the initial session to recognise that we are now all equal members of the group. I also propose that the child tells their parent about music therapy, giving them the role of inviting their parent into the confidentiality of the sessions. Most parents feel a little nervous about playing, so I typically suggest a simple musical game to break the ice. This structure can help everyone in the room to feel a little more relaxed.

In our first session, Susie literally drowned out both Mrs S and me by drumming as loudly as she could while smiling at her mum. She filled the room with sound, the power of her playing seeming to shock and paralyse Mrs S. I sat quietly, allowing Susie to continue. After four minutes, she stopped and announced, 'That was angry music.' There were many ways to interpret her musical behaviour, but, above all, I felt Susie was addressing her mother with the message, 'I'm angry about things and I need you to hear me and know this!' It was crucial to model acceptance of her emotion, not to silence it, so I simply commented, 'I wonder if you were playing angry music because you are feeling angry about something.' Susie smiled and nodded, but did not speak about this further.

I suggested that we play a 'copying game', wishing to observe how mother and daughter played together. Mrs S was keen to play, making up clear rhythmic patterns on the drum for us to copy. When Susie was the leader, she pointed out her mother's mistakes in a scornful voice. Mrs S simply smiled, which reminded me of Susie's constant smile in her initial sessions. Susie made up impossibly long patterns and I eventually pointed this out, commenting that she was not being very fair. I sensed that Mrs S was relieved when I said something. Through her music, Susie clearly expressed some strong feelings towards her mother and I felt that she was trying to provoke any reaction other than the fond smile.

When the game ended, Mrs S started to talk, mentioning how difficult she found Susie's behaviour and lack of respect. She then spoke of her husband's death, explaining that she had wanted him to be buried here where she could visit his grave with Susie, but his family had insisted that he be buried in Portugal. In distress and retaliation, she had subsequently ended all communication with his family, with whom she and Susie had previously been close. Since then, she had felt totally alone as her own family lived in Portugal. As Mrs S talked, I was reminded of Susie's song in our earlier sessions, about the little girl who strangled every member of her extended family, sensing that there was a link between this and the tale of her father's family.

Mrs S talked of how she and her husband had longed for a baby and how delighted they had been when Susie finally arrived. She said her husband was particularly distressed to see his daughter spending so much time in hospital because of her dislocated hip. Tears poured silently down Mrs S's cheeks as she explained that Susie had her final operation two months before her father was killed and, tragically, he never saw her walk.

While Mrs S talked, Susie looked around the room, swinging on her chair, seemingly oblivious to what was being said, smiling whenever she caught my eye. She had not been looking at her mum, but as I now reached out to Mrs S, covering her hand with my hand, Susie glanced round noticing her mum's tears. This seemed to be her cue to cry as she immediately opened her mouth wide and started to howl dramatically. Mother and daughter simply looked at each other and cried for a few seconds, seemingly unsure of what to do in their shared distress. After a few moments, Mrs S shut down her emotion and smiling said, 'Silly mummy. There's nothing wrong. Everything's fine now.' Susie instantly stopped howling, too.

It was striking that neither Susie nor her mother reached out to one another to give comfort or seek comfort. I gestured to Susie to go to her mum, which she did, climbing on her knee for a cuddle. I gently said, 'Actually, everything is not fine. Something terribly sad has happened to both of you and you miss daddy very, very much. I'm sure that it does sometimes make you feel like crying.' I sensed that Mrs S did not want to upset her daughter and she seemed to be communicating that a 'stiff upper lip' was in order and there was no room for tears. I wondered whether she was ashamed or embarrassed about her own tears, whether she was afraid of losing control once she 'opened the floodgates' or whether she simply found it distressing to see her child cry. Mrs S then revealed, 'Susie only saw me cry once at the time of her father's death and it caused her to cry and cling to me so much, I felt it traumatised her further. I felt so guilty about upsetting her, I never cried in front of her again.' I gently suggested that she didn't need to hide that from Susie, as it is all right for children and grown-ups to cry at sad things, especially when they miss someone so precious so much. Mrs S agreed and wept again. Looking up and noticing this, Susie instantly started to howl once more.

The way Susie mirrored her mother was striking. I felt that she needed to access her own feelings about her father's absence from her life. I asked them what they remembered about daddy and they started to recall mostly amusing stories. As Mrs S spoke, tears filled her eyes, but she continued to smile or laugh at their memories. Susie watched her closely, but did not cry again. Mrs S admitted that she had never really spoken to anyone about what had happened or allowed herself to grieve properly. In shutting down her expression of grief, she seemed to have shut down the ability to show any negative emotion to her daughter, including anger.

I suggested that we make up some music whilst thinking about Mr S. Susie seemed truly connected to her emotions when she expressed herself through music. She could now vent her anger intentionally through playing, recognising it and where it stemmed from. Since music seemed to be the key for her to access real emotion, I wanted her to have the opportunity to link feeling with what we had just spoken about. As we played together, the music seemed very poignant and sad, despite the funny anecdotes they had just shared. Afterwards, Susie seemed quiet and vulnerable. I recognised this, linking it to her father, and suggested that Mrs S take her home for the rest of the day, where they could spend special time together, thinking about what we had shared this morning. This was clearly a turning point for Susie in our therapeutic process, where experience, music and feeling became linked in a form that she could hold on to.

We spoke no more of Mr S in the weeks that followed; instead, taking turns to choose activities for the group to share. I introduced this structure, ensuring that Susie did not always pick first and that Mrs S had a chance to assert her own choices and stick to them, rather than giving in to her daughter. Susie and I both chose musical activities, such as improvisation or games, whilst Mrs S always opted to spend some time talking about incidents where she and Susie had clashed at home. It sounded as though Susie continually got her own way, wearing her mother out with her angry outbursts and hurtful comments.

Through the introduction of certain activities and games, Susie and her mother were able to return to an early stage of mother–child play and interaction. I felt it was important to create the opportunity for them to share something light-hearted and fun together, far removed from their usual battles over bedtime and other behaviour at home. Through sharing such experiences, I hoped that Mrs S could enjoy and focus on the positive aspects of their relationship.

Winnicott (1971, p.44) proposes that, 'psychotherapy takes place in the overlap of two areas of playing, that of the patient and that of the therapist'. He goes on to say, 'if the patient cannot play, then something needs to be done to enable the patient to become able to play, after which [psycho] therapy may begin' (Winnicott 1971, p.63). He believes that a child's capacity to play comes out of their relationship with their mother and that play promotes health. In family therapy, music is effective in bringing parents and children together, facilitating play. Oldfield (1999, p.197) writes, 'It [music therapy] can provide an opportunity for the parent and the child to re-experience (or experience for the first time) the early mother–baby types of playful interactions.' Oldfield (1992, 1994, 1999, 2002) demonstrates this in videos of her work with children and their parents. Music not only offers the adult an acceptable medium to play through, but an excuse to play and a shared experience in a containing environment. Indeed, music can be very playful and humorous, allowing a parent to get in touch with their child. Conversely, the child can enjoy finding a way to play with their parent. Both play and music have a communicative function and the dynamics arising from this within the music therapy session are extremely useful to the therapist and can be worked through.

Through the subtlety and safety of improvisation and musical games, Mrs S and Susie expressed deeper feelings towards one another, both consciously and subconsciously. I felt that Susie continued to test her mother, trying to provoke a strong, authoritative response from her. Mrs S was visibly affected by this, looking increasingly fatigued and hurt with each comment or action. She continued to cover her emotions with a kind smile to her daughter whenever their eyes met; however, she would then look down at her lap with a strained expression. Through her body language and playing, Mrs S was actually communicating more of her inner thoughts than she seemed to realise and I felt that Susie picked up on this.

In our eighth session, Susie yelled rudely at Mrs S, who did nothing. I stepped in, expressing shock at the way Susie had spoken to her mother. Modelling ways of relating to the child for the parent's benefit and vice versa is often core to this family work, although this is usually very subtle. On this occasion, I was not subtle and I wondered how Mrs S would feel about me reprimanding her child. She made no comment, sitting back on her chair looking a little relieved. In time, Mrs S gradually responded to my modelling, asserting herself more when dealing with Susie.

I was struck by Oldfield's use of the idea of modelling, which I once heard her describe in a lecture. Within sessions it would be inappropriate to criticise a parent's interaction with their child overtly, especially since they might have very low self-esteem or feel defensive. It is therefore sometimes preferable to allow them to develop their skills through more subtle means, the therapist hoping that they will adopt the techniques she models and how she handles situations, negotiates with or responds to the child. If a parent does copy her behaviour, she might take the opportunity delicately to reinforce their actions as positive. As mentioned, this technique often plays a part in my work with families. For example, in sessions with a parent who constantly talks over their child, I might look for opportunities to comment to the child, 'I'd really like to know what you think about this' or 'That is a very interesting idea'. Such modelling has been very effective in the past, with parents altering elements of their interaction with their child.

Whilst keeping things light, I encouraged Mrs S not always to let her daughter win competitive games, explaining that life doesn't work like that and children need to learn to cope with losing as well as winning. As Mrs S played instruments, she seemed to find her own musical voice, becoming increasingly comfortable and playing more confidently. She eventually tried to meet her daughter's musical challenges, matching Susie's powerful playing. As Mrs S stood up to her daughter, something shifted in the balance of their relationship. Their playing took on a more shared, receptive quality and Susie visibly responded to her mum's assertiveness, sinking into the role of daughter, accepting her mother's decisions without her original teen-style protestations. Musical play allowed Susie and her mum to try on different characters and experiment in the ways they related and responded to one another.

From tales of their home life, I sensed that Mrs S was beginning to take back control from her daughter, calling the shots on bedtime and when homework needed to be done. Meanwhile, Susie seemed to accept her mother's discipline, increasingly doing as she was told. Mrs S and I broke down Susie's typical daily tasks into bite-sized chunks, with rewards and consequences for each. Mrs S stuck to this system, making the most of her new-found control as she recognised that Susie depended on her for rewards such as going swimming.

Having attended music therapy for a term and a half, Mrs S shared that she had been looking at different primary schools in the area with a view to giving Susie a fresh start. She felt that Susie had changed, but she would never escape the label of being a challenging child in our school. Within weeks, Susie had a place at a new, smaller primary school and she was excited about the prospect of moving and being her 'new self' and making new friends. Having worked with Susie for over two years, I felt that she and her mum were ready to move on and a fresh start would do her good.

Ending

As we drew our music therapy sessions to an end, I reflected on the changes in Mrs S, Susie and their relationship. Their patterns of behaviour towards one another had altered dramatically as they had adopted more archetypical mother–daughter roles. Although they had always spoken openly about Mr S's death, they were now able to attach emotion to it, expressing how much they missed him and how they felt about his absence, including sadness or anger that he was taken from them, both by his killers and his family who had insisted on his burial in Portugal. Music therapy had offered them a unique opportunity for self-expression through a medium that they could share safely, whilst maintaining their own identities. Through this, they had been able to internalise and accept their own and one another's feelings, later talking about them together. They had also been able to address the balance of their relationship through the subtlety of musical improvisation and games.

Conclusion

Involving a parent or other family members in a child's music therapy process can often enhance the work, meaning that particular difficulties within relationships can be addressed directly. It is particularly useful working in a child's mainstream school since the safe, non-threatening, child-friendly and child-centred nature of schools, in particular primary schools, can touch parents, leading them to feel more comfortable with this form of support for their child and even themselves. Some parents cannot wait for the opportunity to engage with the large array of instruments and it can be very moving to see a parent playing a tune from their childhood on an instrument they have not seen for some time, especially those native to their homeland abroad. Some parents are quite nervous about playing music, not sure where or how to start. It can be useful to work through this, in terms of observing the child's response to their parent's vulnerability and providing a starting block from which to build the parent's self-confidence among other things.

Play has a major role in music therapy with families. Music facilitates play and this can attract parents to this form of therapeutic support, enhancing the experience for them. It is beneficial to both those who already enjoy playing with their child and those who are struggling to find ways of connecting with their child. On the occasions when a family has rediscovered how to share a game and enjoy playing together, I have observed it to be a significant turning point in the therapy and in their relationships.

In the case of Susie and Mrs S, I hoped that their repressed, unvoiced feelings would surface through their music and play. However, for those parents and children in the midst of dealing with a traumatic experience, music therapy can provide some respite from thinking about their difficulties. There are times when I feel that families desperately need to experience some form of positive, healthy and, above all, light-hearted interaction away from their worries. Through a shared musical improvisation or musical game, they have such an opportunity and this can be beneficial.

The decision to take a child's therapy in this new direction is not taken lightly and many factors require careful consideration and reflection before this decision is made. It has been fortunate that the mainstream primary schools where I work have collaborated warmly in enabling this particular area of practice to develop.

Giving families the chance to vent their feelings, often towards one another, through the subtlety and safety of music can be very useful. This may or may not lead to an open discussion about what was felt. The musical expression and containment can be enough in itself to help individuals move forward within their relationships, coming to terms with how they feel or leaving their emotion behind. Although this chapter has focused on work with one particular individual and her mother, it is possible to see how beneficial it is to offer this service within an environment in which the client already feels secure, and how powerful a therapeutic tool music can be for those who have suffered trauma.

Chapter 7

It's a Family Affair
Music Therapy for Children and Families at a Psychiatric Unit

Emma Davies

Introduction

Working with children and their families together in music therapy is a valuable and effective intervention, particularly within the field of mental health. As the family therapist, G.G. Barnes, explained:

> People in families are intimately connected, and focusing on those connections and the beliefs different members hold about them can be a more valid way of understanding and promoting change in problem-related behaviour than focusing on the perspective of any one individual. (Barnes 1998, p.3).

The aim of this chapter is to show how beneficial it can be to work with children and their families in music therapy and to address difficulties within the context of the family together. We consider how therapeutic aims may be addressed and how this influences the way to approach this work; this information is presented not only in my own words but also in the words of the children and families who are undergoing the therapy. Some of the methods and ideas that are effective with this client group are discussed and we demonstrate how they are put into practice, illustrating them with two case studies.

Two case studies were chosen in particular: first, because they illustrate the way music therapy helped to strengthen two very fragile relationships and brought about positive changes and, second, because they describe work with fathers, about whom there seems to be very little written. The majority of music therapy literature and research focuses on work with mothers and children (Bunt 2002; Nocker-Ribaupierre 1999; Oldfield and Bunce 2001; Warwick 1995), drawing on the theories of Winnicott, Bowlby, Stern and Trevarthen, which highlight the significance of early mother–infant interactions. However, there is very little literature which considers the father–child relationship, and it is important to acknowledge both parental roles.

The setting

The Croft Children's Unit is an inpatient psychiatric unit, based in Cambridge, that provides assessment, diagnosis and treatment for children up to the age of 13. Many of the children admitted have complex emotional, behavioural and developmental disorders, including attachment and conduct disorders, psychosomatic illnesses and neurodevelopment disorders such as autistic spectrum conditions or Asperger syndrome. In most cases children are admitted residentially with their families for a six-week assessment, although occasionally this will be extended. Parenting assessments are also carried out in partnership with social services. Families are admitted as a whole in order to allow the multi-disciplinary team to gain a global view of the difficulties, and to understand the child within the context of their family. This approach forms an integral part of the work of music therapist, Amelia Oldfield (1993, 2006a; Oldfield and Bunce 2001) who has been developing the service for over 20 years. I have worked at the Croft for seven years; for the first three I worked as a research assistant for Oldfield's PhD (2004) as well as taking on her clinical work. During this time I worked with many families on a short-term basis (three or four sessions) whilst they were staying at the Croft. Although some families clearly benefited from short-term music therapy during their admission, there were others who needed further in-depth work once they had been discharged. Yet there was no service to which families could be referred. After providing evidence to prove the efficacy of having an outpatient music therapy service – which included collating parental and staff feedback and giving presentations within the NHS service – I was able to secure funding for a new post. I now work for one day a week providing long-term therapy (up to two years) for children and their families once they have been discharged from the Croft. Although some of this work involves the whole family – child, parents, siblings, grandparents – most focuses on one relationship within the family – child and one parent, step-parent or carer.

Rationale for working with child and parent together

For many of the families attending the Croft Children's Unit life has become extremely difficult and stressful. An admission may be the culmination of years of appointments, assessments and numerous interventions with different professionals. For some, the Croft can represent a 'last chance' before more drastic measures are considered, such as placing a child into care. For those who receive a clear diagnosis for their child, there may be a sense of relief. In some cases medication can prove effective, as may the offer of specialised educational placements. However, a diagnosis does not always act as a magic wand; indeed, some families struggle to deal with the implications of diagnosis. Those for whom no diagnosis is given need to come to terms with the fact that it may be family dynamics that are exacerbating their child's difficulties, rather than some external, diagnosable cause. Families may have also become locked into negative interaction patterns and need support to rediscover positive ways of interacting, and this is where music therapy can play a significant role.

Case studies

The following case studies illustrate how music therapy helped to strengthen the relationships between two children and their fathers and how it can reinforce existing bonds and develop new ones. Afterwards, my approach is explored in greater detail by discussing how music therapy can address specific therapeutic aims.

Jamie and Mark

Jamie was ten when he was referred to the Croft Children's Unit with severe behavioural and social problems. His behaviour could be very unpredictable, often ending in violent outbursts, and he had great difficulties regulating his emotions. He had been struggling to cope in mainstream school (and in fact he had recently been excluded permanently) and there was generally a great deal of concern over his future. Jamie was admitted to the Croft with his family to help identify the main issues and triggers to his behaviour and to look at what support they might need.

During the two and a half months' admission it became clear that family dynamics were playing a significant part in Jamie's difficulties. His parents, Clare and Mark, were separated and Jamie lived with his mother and two younger sisters. There was very little contact between Mark and the children and one of Jamie's main concerns was that he might lose contact altogether.

Both Clare and her mother (Jamie's grandmother) were very negative about Mark and attempted to discourage his involvement. At this point Mark was finding it very difficult to establish a role for himself in the family.

Jamie's first involvement with music therapy was in the weekly group run by Amelia Oldfield. She noted his enthusiasm and ability to be musically creative. She also observed that he responded well to praise and was willing to give instruments a try, even if he perceived them as being difficult. This was surprising as Jamie's typical response in this situation had been to reject something he could not succeed at immediately. At this point it was felt by the team that Jamie could benefit from some individual work for the remainder of his admission with the view to continuing it after his discharge. I therefore started to see him for weekly sessions.

It was clear from the first session that Jamie was extremely musical and had a natural talent for improvisation. He demonstrated a sensitivity in his playing, particularly at the piano, which was surprising in a ten-year-old child. He quickly made links with music and his feelings and identified instruments for different moods. For example, he chose percussion when he wanted to play loudly and 'let off steam' or the piano when he wanted to be quieter and more reflective. Despite all the reports of his unpredictable and out-of-control behaviour, Jamie never displayed any of it in the music room. He was always keen to come to his session and engage in music-making. However, I did notice that although his playing was confident, he frequently asked me whether his music was 'OK' or 'good' and whether we would be having another session. He seemed to need my approval as well as reassurance that he could trust me.

During the discharge meeting, at the end of the admission, I was able to feed back to Jamie's parents how well Jamie had engaged in music therapy and how he had started to make good use of his time to explore using music to express himself. I also explained that he was actually very talented, which they clearly found very encouraging. We all felt that the work should continue with the aim of eventually involving Mark. The family's admission at the Croft had instigated some positive changes and Mark was increasingly playing a more active role within the family. I felt that attending music therapy could help strengthen Jamie and Mark's relationship by providing a regular opportunity to spend time together. For the next year, Mark brought Jamie to the Croft every week.

Initially, Jamie asked if he could participate in music therapy on his own. I was very aware, however, that Mark might feel excluded by being outside the music room during the session. I felt torn between wanting to continue providing a safe and confidential space for Jamie, and involving Mark. I was aware of how excluded Mark felt in relation to the family situation and did not want to exacerbate this. As the music therapist Simon Procter (2005) explains '[there may exist] a tension between therapists' dual concerns, on the one hand, to preserve confidentiality and, on the other, to inform and support parents'. However, in this case the situation resolved itself when Jamie, after several months, asked whether his dad could join us for the second half of the session.

Naturally, adding a third person to a situation changes the dynamics and I was a little nervous of how they would both feel. At times Jamie was very keen to show Mark the instruments and explain what we had been doing and at other times he seemed quite cut off, engrossed in his own playing, and there was very little interaction between them. Mark seemed anxious and unsure how to play. He tended to play quietly as if he did not want to take up too much space and, like Jamie, he seemed to need my reassurance. At this point I felt very much in between them, trying to bring them together, trying to instil musical confidence in both by reflecting and developing elements of their playing within my own. After one very quiet and reflective improvisation Mark commented that he found the experience 'therapeutic'. I wondered whether he was responding to the experience of being listened to and accepted, which perhaps he had not felt for some time. I wanted them both to feel that music therapy was a non-judgemental environment in which they both felt they could 'risk' trying out ideas.

During these early sessions I felt that it was important to introduce an element of structured playing as well as free improvisation. This helped maintain a focus and prevented the session from being disjointed. For example, I suggested that we take it in turns to lead the playing, create a musical story with sound effects, improvise around a rhythm that Jamie or Mark initiated or choose a theme or mood for an improvisation (as Jamie had done in his individual sessions).

As we experimented with different styles and instruments, Mark and Jamie became more relaxed with each other. Mark talked about his past musical experiences and surprised Jamie by saying that he used to play the guitar. This generated a shared interest in the guitar and they enjoyed improvising duets, supported by me on percussion. I wondered whether, by boosting Mark's self-esteem and acknowledging that his contribution to the sessions was valuable, he would gain a sense of belonging and purpose which could enable him to feel a more confident and available father for Jamie.

As the sessions progressed Mark and Jamie explored many different ways of interacting and playing together. They clearly enjoyed each other's company and it seemed that music had become something special between them. Mark clearly felt immense pride as Jamie developed into a very accomplished musician. A music teacher at his school had noticed him and began to give him drum lessons. Mark bought him a drum kit and guitar, and Jamie's mum acquired a piano for the home. Jamie played at the Croft annual fête and brought his family, friends and school teachers to hear him. Music was becoming a significant part of Jamie's life.

I started to realise that music therapy had achieved what it had set out to do and that it was therefore time to bring it to an end. This was a difficult decision as the sessions had become so enjoyable, but it was important to acknowledge that we no longer needed to bring Jamie and Mark together each week because they were now spending regular time together. The relationship between Mark and Jamie's mother was much better and Mark had moved to a house very nearby. Jamie and Mark's relationship had become much more secure and it really seemed that Mark had finally found his place as being a central figure in Jamie's life.

In the last session Jamie asked his dad to improvise at the piano with him while I listened. As the music developed they picked up on each other's music, reflecting rhythms or melodic fragments. I remember feeling very moved by this and thinking that they now had the skills and shared experience to ensure that music-making remained something meaningful and special between them into the future.

I asked both Jamie and Mark to write something about their experiences of music therapy (their feedback questionnaires are included at the end of this chapter).

Music therapy from Mark's perspective:

I would portray myself as reserved and bordering on shy, whilst my son, Jamie, is the opposite. He gets stuck into new situations and surroundings with vigour. However, at the time he first started music therapy, he also had a tendency to give up in frustration if tasks became difficult. Also his behaviour was erratic and unpredictable.

When Jamie was asked if he would like to extend his music therapy sessions, he was very keen to do so, and was counting on me to come

along. Our first session was both moving and challenging. I was immediately aware that Jamie was looking to me for my approval and
attention. While accompanying Jamie and Emma on a variety of percussion and stringed instruments, giving my attention was easy as I was
amazed by his musical ability.

The situation was challenging because I did not want to expose my
musical inability. When I have helped Jamie with his homework, he
would lose interest very quickly and become distracted as soon as he
found a piece of schoolwork difficult. During music therapy sessions he
worked through his mistakes creatively so as not to lose his momentum.

As the sessions went on, both Jamie and I looked forward to experimenting with different instruments and playing in a variety of styles. I
find that I have become less self-conscious and Jamie has gained my
respect in an area of ability that I would not have been aware of had we
not attended music therapy with Emma.

Jamie's thoughts:

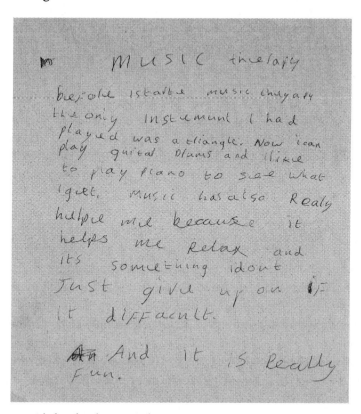

Figure 7.1 Jamie's thoughts about music therapy

From the perspective of Vince Hesketh (family therapist):

> When Jamie was admitted to the Croft with his mother and two sisters, Mark had become detached from the family despite living two miles from the family home. Jamie's mother insisted that Mark would not get involved and yet he was immediately interested in participating as soon as staff members made direct contact with him. This began the rekindling of the relationship between Mark and his family and it could be argued that Jamie's behaviour had escalated in order to re-involve his father.
>
> Mark's own childhood was very traumatic. He was certainly not listened to. The immediate therapy allowed Mark to experience being heard but without the use of words, whilst allowing the father–son dyad to try new ways of relating. Not only did this heal the relationship between Jamie and his dad but it also allowed Mark to repair some of the struggle he had with his own father.
>
> Therapy with Jamie's family focused on re-involving his father and encouraging him to take his rightful position as co-parent within a separated marriage – a role that had been taken by Jamie's maternal grandmother.

Katie and John

Katie was 13 when she was admitted to the Croft with a history of anxiety and depressive disorder. Despite being a very bright and capable student, she had started to refuse to attend school and her parents were struggling to manage the situation. The aim of the admission was to assess Katie's difficulties by looking at how the whole family functioned and to support a programme of school reintegration.

Katie was extremely close to her mother, describing her as her 'best friend,' but appeared to have a very difficult relationship with her father. John was an older father, in his fifties, and presented as a very smart, rather formal man who described himself as having a reputation for maintaining standards of order and punctuality. He seemed very frustrated by what he perceived as Katie's rebelliousness and disobedience. Katie seemed to find her father old-fashioned and strict. Their relationship seemed disconnected and stuck.

By the end of the admission Katie was reasonably well settled into a new school. However, the team felt that she needed further support to help develop and strengthen the relationship with her father. Katie had engaged well in the music therapy group during her admission and had expressed an interest in continuing with further work. In addition John was musical and they both had attended lessons in the past. Music seemed an ideal medium through which to work and so they were referred for weekly outpatient sessions.

Before music therapy commenced I talked to John about how it might work and what his expectations were. He talked positively about music but mentioned his disappointment at Katie's lack of discipline with her music practice. He seemed surprised when I explained that the sessions would involve improvisation and would not necessarily follow a structured plan. Despite his hesitancy he was nevertheless motivated to give it a try.

John arrived at their first session with an armful of piano books and suggested that we all try out some of the pieces. I felt an initial pang of frustration, as it seemed he had not taken my explanation of music therapy theory on board. I then wondered whether I was experiencing his feelings of frustration with Katie. When I suggested we improvise together he seemed to find this concept very difficult, preferring instead to play familiar melodies. I wondered what purpose the music books and the melodies served for John. Were they being used as a defence or as a way of avoiding something uncomfortable? Katie, in stark contrast to her father, took a much more spontaneous and free approach to music-making and I was struck by how confident her playing seemed in comparison to how anxious she had appeared initially. She seemed frustrated by her father's preference for clear structure. By observing the contrasting ways that Katie and John approached music-making, it was clear that their general differences had become a source of mutual resentment. I wondered whether music therapy could help them find some common ground so that they could reconnect and begin to enjoy interacting with each other.

STRUCTURE VERSUS SPONTANEITY

During the first few sessions I often felt very stuck between Katie and John as I tried to strike a balance between their musical differences. When we played pre-composed pieces, I tried to engage Katie, who seemed uninterested. During free improvisations I tried to connect musically with John, who tended to become lost in trying to establish a key or rhythm while Katie seemed deliberately to play against her father. They did not listen to one other, and the music simply served to highlight the sense of disconnection between them. After one improvisation in which I had tried to incorporate both of their melodic phrasing within my own in an effort to bring them together, I asked them both to describe how they felt during the playing. Katie said that she felt her dad was not listening to her – but that she wanted him to. John described feeling as if he was in his 'own cocoon' but that he had been trying to follow us. Feelings of isolation and a need to be heard and valued were significant themes being explored in their family therapy at the time so it was not surprising these were being reflected in the music.

SPONTANEITY WITHIN STRUCTURE

I started to introduce a variety of musical ideas to encourage Katie and John to listen to each other and to experience and accept each other's musical preferences without it feeling threatening. For example, I suggested we each take it in turns to play a set rhythm or melodic line over which the others could improvise freely. This activity provided the opportunity to be sponta- neous within the security of an overall structure, thus appealing to both their needs. We also took turns 'conducting', which involved careful following of different beats. John was very positive about his 'orchestra' (Katie and me) commenting that it was very 'responsive'. They started to be more playful in their attempts to 'catch' each other out with quickly contrasting tempi. I also encouraged them to choose a theme or mood for an improvisation so as to provide a focus. Although their choices were very different (Katie suggested 'quiet and dreamy', John: 'Bach-like and then Beethoven'), they nevertheless started to take up one other's ideas. John commented after one such themed improvisation that Katie and he were more 'in sync' with each other.

As the sessions progressed John became more relaxed and focused less on playing in the 'correct' way. I noticed that he no longer brought his music books. It seemed that he had needed the reassurance or permission to venture away from the expected and to experiment with musical elements. I wondered whether he experienced spontaneity or unconventionality as something difficult as it exposed him and left him vulnerable. Yet it was at these times that Katie responded most to her father. When he commented that he was 'spoiling' the music, she gave him encouragement.

Katie asked whether she could improvise with me on her own while her dad listened. Initially I feared this may increase John's sense of isolation but actually he thoroughly enjoyed listening to his daughter. Katie was able to improvise in a very musical and sensitive way, and he clearly felt immense pride in her ability. Katie, in turn, gained her father's praise and approval, which seemed to help her be more flexible when it came to playing in his stylistic choice. I also think it helped John to observe how I picked up some of Katie's musical ideas and developed them within an improvisation. We began to audiotape these improvisations as they were becoming such a highlight of the sessions.

After six months John and Katie decided together that they would like to finish music therapy. Katie was now attending school without any difficulties and the family felt that they no longer needed the Croft's support. I felt that it was important that the work ended on a positive note so that they would have something enjoyable to look back on. I made a copy of the piano improvisations for them as a reminder of their time together in music therapy. They talked about listening to it together and even trying out duets at home.

A few months after the sessions finished, I sent John and Katie questionnaires (included at the end of this chapter) as I was keen to gain some feedback of their thoughts and memories of music therapy. John identified that music therapy had helped strengthen his relationship with Katie by offering them the opportunity to share something that they both enjoyed, even if it was in different ways. He hoped that the positive experience would continue beyond the end of music therapy and become something that they could share at home. Katie pointed out that she enjoyed the freedom of being able to play instruments that she wouldn't normally play at home with her dad. She also acknowledged that music therapy had helped her to build a better relationship with her dad.

From the perspective of Vince Hesketh (family therapist):

> In contrast to Jamie's family, Katie's father was dominant and rigid in his style of parenting, which infantilised his wife and did not allow the more flexible boundaries needed for Katie to make the transition from childhood to adolescence. Sadly, this dominance left John emotionally isolated from his wife and three children. The music therapy opened a crucial door for John to become more spontaneous in a context that provided just enough containment for him to feel secure. The struggle between spontaneity and structure delightfully mirrors the struggle between the overprotective male over the free-spirited adolescent.

Music therapy had enabled both Katie and John to see one another's differences as something positive rather than as a threat. Their mutual interest in music, combined with a motivation to repair their relationship, helped them to address their difficulties and identify what they needed from each other in a non-confrontational way. It also provided them with the opportunity to explore being spontaneous within a secure and contained space, and to build up enjoyable, shared experiences together. Music was clearly going to continue to be a positive force for their relationship in the future.

My approach in relation to addressing therapeutic aims

As the case studies highlight, music therapy is able to address a variety of therapeutic aims. As each case is unique it is impossible to identify one approach that can be applied to all. Developing a therapeutic relationship with each family and understanding their particular needs are key parts of the work. However, there are some ways of working that have emerged from my clinical practice which I have found particularly useful in working with this client group. These are now explored in relation to addressing therapeutic aims.

Exploring emotions within music

Sometimes children who have great difficulty expressing themselves in conventional ways can use improvised song-singing to convey their feelings to their parents. I have elsewhere described my work with one young teenager with severe emotional and behavioural problems who, in addition, found it very difficult to express himself owing to poor articulation (Davies 2005). This young man talked about wanting to tell his mother the issues that he was struggling with at the time but that he found it a challenge do so. By working with them together and providing a space for them to try out different ways of expressing themselves through music, we eventually discovered that he had a real aptitude for rapping. He was then able to communicate his feelings to his mother by 'singing' (rap-style) rather than speaking. In this way their relationship was able to move on and become more positive.

In this case the teenager asked us simply to listen to him, but there are other times when the parent and I become more musically involved. For example, I might play a steady beat on a percussion instrument while the child tries out different sung phrases. After a while the parent can take up this 'rhythmic role' while I use the flexibility that this improvisatory technique creates to reinforce musically on another instrument certain phrases, both of the child's singing and the parent's playing. In this way the child can explore feelings within the safety of this structure while the parent can experience both being supported (by me) and supporting the child. As the case study highlights, the aim is to help the parent gain confidence, which it is hoped may be incorporated into the parent–child relationship beyond the therapy room.

Although this way of using the song structures can be a useful tool, singing does not come naturally to everyone; in fact, for some it can be an excruciating experience, so I only ever suggest it as one among other possible ideas. I may also propose that we improvise freely together and then talk afterwards about how the music made us feel. Or, if this idea is too abstract and a more structured approach is required, we may take it in turns to play some music with a specific feeling in mind. One child suggested that we create a competition in which we each had to guess the feeling portrayed in each other's music. He even devised a points system to score how successful each one of us had been.

Some children enjoy involving their parents in improvised musical stories. They may ask the parent to tell the story while they provide the sound effects. Finger puppets can be a useful resource in this situation, especially for younger children, who may use them to symbolise different feelings or to communicate something indirectly to their parents. One child decided that her little owl puppet was going to be 'sad' while her mum's elephant puppet was to be 'cross'. I was instructed to play appropriate music for each. At the end of the story I asked the owl whether it wanted to say anything to the elephant. It said, 'Tell me that you are not angry any more', which the mother was able to do through the elephant. Observing and analysing the way that children use these improvised stories can help give insight into the child's inner world and how they perceive relationships with others (Oldfield and Franke 2005). I see my role as providing both the parents and children with tools and ideas to help them communicate and, ultimately, bring about positive change.

There are some families who find it too challenging to address their difficulties by talking together, and therefore may not yet be ready to engage in family or other verbal therapy. In such cases it is important to reassure them that music therapy is simply a space in which they can play music without any pressure to talk. It may be that issues arise in the sessions that we can address by talking but the focus will be on the music. One child, with behavioural and some learning difficulties, and his father, with a communication disorder, found it difficult to interact verbally but they were able to do so through music. They enjoyed playing musical games and often asked to be taught melodies at the piano. As the sessions progressed I introduced the idea of playing music to portray different emotions. They took this idea up readily, in particular expressing anger by playing as loudly as possible. In this way they were able to use music as an outlet for feelings that they could not verbalise. Music therapy, therefore, can support families in identifying and expressing emotions which previously may have been too demanding an experience. This can instigate the first step to addressing problems which, when the family is ready, may be solved in verbal therapy.

Issues of control

Music therapy can be a useful space for exploring the issues of control in a creative and non-verbal way. Controlling behaviour can have a negative effect on the way families interact and it can manifest itself in different ways. In one case a boy was extremely controlling over when his mother played music and what she played. He screamed at her if she played in what he perceived as 'the wrong way' and found it very difficult to allow any kind of spontaneous play to occur. However, he did respond to clear structure and liked things to be fair. I suggested we take turns to lead each other's music, following different rhythms, stops and starts. I wondered whether the child needed to experience his mother really listening to him and whether his controlling behaviour served to force her to do so. He engaged well in this activity and delighted in bringing the music to a sudden stop to see if he could catch us out. The fact that he enjoyed this game enabled him, later on, to tolerate his mother being the leader, which helped him experience not being in control as something manageable and non-threatening.

Of course it is not just children who display controlling behaviour. For some parents maintaining control can be the only way to discipline their children's unpredictable behaviour and, possibly, avoid dealing with diffi-culties over the emotional side of their relationship. It can be helpful for the parent to see how I interact with their child, which may be in a boundaried but creative way. I can model different ways of dealing with difficult behaviour, such as channelling it into music-making or using distraction techniques. These methods, in conjunction with parenting strategies and psycho-emotional support provided by the multi-disciplinary team, will be continued and developed outside therapy and, it is hoped, start the process of developing healthier, functioning family relationships.

Strengthening the parent–child bond

As both case studies describe, sometimes the relationship between a child and parent has become very fragile and both parties may need support to rediscover confidence in each other. Bringing them together regularly in music therapy and helping them to build up shared experiences through music-making can help to repair that bond. As the work with Jamie and Mark demonstrates, if a child and parent are struggling to communicate, encouraging them to try musical 'conversations' can ease the pressure and may result in interesting and sometimes poignant moments. For example, I worked with one mother and son who had a very turbulent relationship. Neither seemed to be able to say the right thing to the other and they were very quick to reject each other. My initial response in this case was to work with the child alone as I felt he needed time away from his mother. He engaged very well and I then thought it would be more useful to involve his mother and address some of their difficulties together. During one session I asked them if there was anything they would like to say to each other. The child picked up two animal castanets and gave one to his mum. They started to 'talk' to each other by tapping out different rhythms. I wondered aloud what the two animals were saying to each other. The child said, 'This animal is saying "I love you, Mummy".' The mother responded by saying 'I love you, too, you know.' These sentiments, which they both needed to hear, were somehow easier to express through the act of playing an instrument. Perhaps it felt more comfortable and less risky to express feelings in this indirect way. By the time the music therapy came to an end, they appeared to have a much more positive attitude towards each other. They had also discovered a mutual interest in music which they talked about exploring in the future.

Music can provide a natural resource when working with parents and babies. Different ways of interacting and playing can be modelled without it feeling patronising or embarrassing for the parent because the focus is on the baby and the music. Parents can be encouraged to play, sing or gently rock the baby whilst nursery songs are played. Oldfield and Bunce (2001) describe how a music therapy group for young mothers helped to establish successful bonding between parent and child by providing the opportunity to experience being playful and enjoy their children's responses to music-making.

Increasing self-esteem and confidence: a two-way process

The process that many of the parents undergo – of intense observation and assessment – may bring about feelings of powerlessness and a lack of self-confidence in parenting ability. By creating opportunities where both child and parent can be praised, self-esteem may be improved and thus produce a positive 'ripple-effect' beyond therapy and into family life, especially if this is the first positive thing that has been identified in a long time. Some parents comment that they feel a sense of relief that a 'professional' is able to see positives in their child. Sometimes a real musical talent in a child may be discovered (as the first case study described), which can result in a sense of achievement. Some children enjoy playing the role of teacher with their parent. This can enable them to feel that they, too, have skills that they can share. A mother commented once that her son had a much more positive and flexible attitude to learning after attending music therapy. She felt that this was partly because his self-confidence had been increased through learning to play different instruments and simple piano pieces. The fact that she clearly felt proud of her son, despite his difficulties, seemed to strengthen their relationship and boosted her confidence as a parent.

Beyond the therapy room

It is often useful to video sessions, not only to help to evaluate work but also as a way of recording positive moments for children and their families to keep. This can be especially important when music therapy finishes. A DVD, video or CD creates a permanent reminder of the enjoyment and achievements that a family may have experienced in music therapy, which can help maintain the benefits of therapy into the future. Some children are keen to video a song or musical story that they have created with their parent and want to show it to the rest of the family and friends. This can provide the opportunity for a child who may have hitherto been perceived as 'difficult' to be seen in a more positive light and thus continue to gain praise and self-confidence. I see music therapy as having a valuable effect not just in the duration of the therapy but beyond the music room into families' lives.

Conclusion

This chapter has demonstrated how valuable it can be to work with children and their families in music therapy. For many of the families at the Croft, life has become extremely difficult and stressful, and some have reached the point where they are no longer able to talk or interact positively together.

Music therapy can play an important part in increasing self-esteem, thus empowering families with a renewed sense of ability. This type of work therefore offers long-term support and the potential for change in families who have been going through very demanding times.

My role is therefore to provide the opportunity for families to express and process difficult issues within a contained and supportive environment, and to enable them to find their own ways of interacting. Working with children and families may be challenging at times but it is always immensely thought-provoking and rewarding.

Acknowledgement

Thanks are owed to all the families who have allowed me to write about their experiences of music therapy at the Croft and from whom I have learnt so much.

Feedback questionnaire: parent

I would like to find out what you thought about the music therapy sessions you attended at the Croft. By telling me what you think, you can help other people understand how music therapy can be beneficial.

None of these questions *need* to be answered – if they help you that's fine – but don't feel they need to be answered. Feel free to write as much or as little as you want to.

1. Perhaps a paragraph or two about your initial concerns about your son/daughter, his/her particular strengths and difficulties and also what you particularly enjoy about him/her.

2. Why did you think your son/daughter would benefit from music therapy? How do you use music at home?

3. First impressions about music therapy? Any particular concerns?

4.   What did you feel like being in the music therapy? Was it like anything you have experienced before?

5.   What have *you* particularly enjoyed about the sessions?

6.   Do you think your son/daughter benefited from the sessions and if so, can you explain?

7.   Do you think it was important to be in the same room with your son/daughter during the sessions?

8.   What do you hope for the future in terms of music for you both…?

I understand that the information I give may be included in music therapy presentations and/or literature written by Emma Davies.

Signed:..

Print name:..

All the information you provide will be treated confidentially and all names will be changed. Thank you very much for taking the time to complete this questionnaire.

Feedback questionnaire: child

I would like to find out what you thought about the music therapy sessions you attended at the Croft. By telling me what you think, you can help other people understand how music therapy can be beneficial.

1. How long did you attend music therapy?

2. Who did you attend with?

3. Why do you think you were offered music therapy?

4. What did you like best about your time in the music room?

5. Was there anything you didn't like about the sessions?

6. Have you ever done anything like music therapy before?

7.   Did you like having your mum/dad in your sessions? Can you
       explain why you did or didn't?

8.   Please add any other thoughts.

All of the information you provide will be treated confidentially and all
names will be changed. Thank you for taking the time to complete this questionnaire.

Chapter 8

Music Therapy after Adoption
The Role of Family Music Therapy in Developing Secure Attachment in Adopted Children

Colette E. Salkeld

Introduction

The aim of this chapter is to show the unique role that music therapists can play in the area of care after adoption: using our music within families to enable children with attachment difficulties to build trust in their adoptive parents.

Adopted children who have had a number of attachment and loss experiences in their early lives may experience emotional problems which lead to difficulties in trusting their adoptive parents. Over the past three years I have been working with adoptive families and I hope to demonstrate in this chapter that music therapy has the potential to play a significant role in enabling adopted children to develop secure attachments. Attachment is essentially a reciprocal, two-way process. The case work which will be presented in this chapter will therefore show how working with both the adopted child and their parents together in music therapy, creating space for each member of the family to have a voice, can make a significant contribution to post-adoption support.

In order to carry out this work I am employed privately, receiving referrals from my local post-adoption service. I gave a workshop-style presentation to the post-adoption team, focusing on the value of music therapy as a means of developing secure attachment. After doing this I was referred families whom the team felt might benefit from this type of creative intervention. In order to carry out the clinical work I hired a room and ensured that I liaised regularly with families' adoption social workers, keeping them informed of clinical progress. It was extremely helpful to find a clinical supervisor who was jointly trained as a social worker and psychotherapist.

My clinical work with adoptive families is grounded in attachment theory. In the 1940s and 1950s Bowlby (Bowlby and Ainsworth 1953, 1965) studied the long term developmental effects on children who had been separated from their parents, as war orphans or evacuees, and also on children who had suffered emotional adversity in childhood. In both cases Bowlby believed that the children went on to develop a range of behavioural, emotional and mental health problems. From his analysis of parent–child relationships, and with the help of Ainsworth (Bowlby and Ainsworth 1953, 1965), Bowlby developed attachment theory. Central to his thinking is that a child has to believe that an attachment figure is present both psychologically as well as physically. Bowlby (1988) found that an attachment figure who was physically present and yet emotionally absent could arouse similar feelings of anxiety and distress as an attachment figure who was physically absent. Essentially, for children to thrive they need a close, continuous care-giving relationship: an attachment figure who is available and responsive to their needs.

The very medium at our disposal as music therapists can enable adopted children to find their voice, to express difficult feelings, maybe even for the first time. For many adopted children the trauma that they have experienced may have taken place before they were verbal or they may feel a sense of shame about talking about their experiences. Music therapy, being an essentially non-verbal medium, allows children to go back to these early moments and process their difficult experiences. In addition, the non-verbal nature of music therapy enables adoptive parents to respond to their adopted child in a new way, encouraging the child to value their new family. Adopted children, traumatised from early family life, may never have experienced attachment figures as being available and responsive. Involving their new parents in this process means that this often-painful process can be shared and thought about both within the boundaries of therapy and also in the family. Working in this way enables a child to become more securely attached as they develop trust and security in their adoptive parents. The music therapist acts as the facilitator in building healthy relationships within the family.

Literature

Adoption and trauma literature point to the validity of this approach. Shepperd (2000) writes that individuals process traumatic events in different ways and that the trauma can be responded to by using defence mechanisms such as denial, splitting, regression and isolation. Sometimes feelings are suppressed and this can be reflected in challenging behavioural problems. When looking at individual treatments for traumatised children and adolescents, she writes:

> From an initial family approach the therapeutic needs of individual members which may need addressing in their own right will become apparent; however, a family approach remains essential to utilise the family's resources in helping the child, monitoring progress and addressing dysfunctional behaviours. (Shepperd 2000, p.142)

Howe *et al.* (1999, p.272) argue that 'many of the most effective interventions involve both children and parents who are required jointly to think about, reflect upon and try out behaviours and emotions that are more positive, constructive and supportive'. These authors go on to say that in order for any kind of attachment behaviour to be biologically useful both parties in the bond need to be interested in one another. Working together in therapy clearly enables both the child and the parent to feel that they are jointly interested in one another.

One of the key aims for any clinician in working with adoptive families is to enable them to have fulfilling relationships with one another. Some parents need help to be enabled to be sensitive to the needs of their adopted child, just as if he or she were their birth child.

In writing about attachment, Ainsworth (1973) defines maternal sensitivity as 'the mother's ability and willingness to try and understand behaviours and emotions from her baby's point of view. The result sees a gradual increase in synchrony between parent and child' (p.19). It is within a relationship like this, which is attuned and co-ordinated, that children can learn to regulate their own feelings and behaviours.

Although primarily writing about the relationship between the therapist and the patient, Casement (1985) sheds light upon the role of the music therapist when addressing the need to build healthy attachment in adoptive families. He says that there needs to be someone whose primary role is to be there to support both the mother and the child as they begin to get to know one another:

> If the mother feels adequately held then she is much more likely to be
> able to learn from her baby how best to be the mother which, at that
> moment, her baby most needs her to be. To begin with, this means
> learning her baby's language and individual rhythms. (Casement 1985,
> p.22)

Casement (1985) succinctly describes the process that needs to take place
within an adoptive family in order to develop secure attachments between an
adopted child and the adoptive parents. With both the mother or father and
child present within the therapy the music therapist can support the parent,
enabling him or her to get to know their child. The language that Casement
(1985) uses is innately musical and points to the potential strengths of music
therapy as a medium through which relationships can be built and emotions
shared.

I now briefly describe my music therapy approach with adopted
children and their parents before describing a specific piece of case work in
some detail.

Music therapy approach

When working with younger children I always begin each session with a
greeting song and end each session with a 'Goodbye' song. This creates a
framework to work within. After a particularly difficult session I also believe
that the 'Goodbye' song may bring closure. Within this framework I tend to
take a non-directive approach, which is essentially child-focused and
child-led, using mainly improvised music. By taking this approach children
are allowed to engage in free association through playing with the instruments. Winnicott writes:

> In terms of free association this means that the patient on the couch or
> the child patient among the toys on the floor must be allowed to com-
> municate a succession of ideas, thoughts, impulses, sensations that are
> not linked except in some way that is neurological or physiological.
> (Winnicott 1971, p.55)

In the same way that Winnicott (1971) recognised the importance of the
non-verbal aspect of a child's playing, the non-verbal nature of music
therapy can play a remarkable role in allowing children, through their play,
to show both the therapist and the parent how they need to be communicated with. Observing how they play, and responding musically, can enable a

positive interaction to take place. This is especially true when families have found themselves in negative patterns of interacting and they are unable to recognise the good qualities in one another. I always encourage parents to allow their child to be the starting point and to model what their child does, just as they would do with a tiny baby. Adoptive parents can often find this rather threatening, worrying that they might lose control of their 'difficult' child. When adoptive parents find it uncomfortable to play in this way I may take the lead, modelling to the parent what I mean and showing them the effectiveness of this approach. This process can take time, perhaps weeks or, in some cases, months. The eventual aim, however, is to encourage family members to play with one another. When a parent can play with their child and they can respond to their child's voice, I can then take a step back, supporting and facilitating their new relationship.

A great number of adopted children with attachment problems may never have experienced the nurturing environment of very early mother–baby interactions, such as a mother responding to her baby's babbling. I explain to adoptive parents the non-verbal nature of music therapy and that during a session I will help the family to play with one another through making music. I also talk about the fact that music therapy can sometimes help to recreate early mother–baby interactions, which can enable them to bond with their adopted child. This can be comforting for adoptive parents as it is these earliest experiences that they may never have shared with their adopted child. The music therapy space can recreate this environment and enable adoptive parents and their adopted children to find new ways of relating through musical interactions. In this way the adopted child can experience their emotions as expressed in the music, while being contained musically by the adoptive parents.

Story-telling has become an important part of the music therapy sessions, both in the assessment sessions and in ongoing work. Story-telling may be used to identify attachment difficulties. The clinical psychologist, Franca Brenninkmeyer (2005), presented her findings following a study in this particular area at the 'Attachment in Action' forum. She found that when presented with the beginning of a story children with attachment difficulties found it impossible to make up a happy ending. I therefore always include some form of story-telling, including background music, in the assessment sessions in order to see how the child will respond. A story told in the third person may also be a child's way of indirectly sharing fears or worries

(Oldfield and Franke 2005), which can then be shared with adoptive parents.

Below is a specific piece of case work, described in some detail, to illustrate my music therapy approach.

John

John was five years old when his adoptive parents, Mr and Mrs Smith, and his adoption social worker referred him for music therapy. Mr and Mrs Smith made the referral through their local post-adoption service, after receiving an information sheet on music therapy. At this stage John had been with them for three years. They discussed with their adoption social worker how music therapy might benefit their adopted son and hoped that it would reduce John's violent and angry outbursts, and generally develop his social skills and his ability to trust his adoptive parents.

Having received the referral I went to the family home to meet with Mr and Mrs Smith. John was at school and Mr Smith had taken the day off work. From talking with them it was clear that they felt deeply committed to John, even though they found life with him very difficult. Mr Smith said that if they gave up on him he would have no one else. I was able to take a detailed history from them.

John was severely neglected from birth until the age of nine months. According to social services records he was neglected and understimulated during this time and he also suffered with asthma. John was taken into foster care aged ten months and he remained with the same foster family for one year. Throughout this time he was hospitalised frequently because of his asthma.

John was placed with Mr and Mrs Smith when aged 22 months old and they adopted him ten months later. Mr and Mrs Smith said that it was clear that John had bonded with his foster carer and they described how the move from the foster family was very traumatic. Mrs Smith described how the foster mother was crying loudly, distraught that she was losing John, whilst he showed no emotion at all. Mr and Mrs Smith described him as being emotionally shut down at that time, sitting in the back of the car motionless.

Mr and Mrs Smith said that when they arrived home with John, they were in shock because he was so needy. As John was 22 months old they had expected him to be more self-sufficient. They described him as being an emotionally demanding child, although he was already talking and walking, and they felt unprepared for this. Mrs Smith said that they focused on his medical needs, not feeling prepared for his emotional state. They found his 24-hour neediness very difficult to deal with. Mrs Smith described herself as someone to feed and clothe John rather than someone to mother him. Both she and her husband described how this led to them distancing themselves from him. Mrs Smith went back to work full-time and Mr Smith worked long hours, leaving early and returning home after John was in bed. John was placed in a nursery for five days a week when Mrs Smith returned to work, and his behaviour at home at this time was becoming increasingly aggressive and controlling.

Before their being referred for music therapy Mr and Mrs Smith had attended a course run by their local post-adoption service called 'A Piece of Cake', which is a re-parenting course specifically for adopters when there are problems attaching to their adopted child. It gives parents insight into why their child may be behaving in a particular way and how their style of parenting can help or hinder the healing of past trauma. Having attended the parenting course Mrs Smith felt that her absence at home might be exacerbating their problems with John and as a consequence was now only working part-time.

In our discussion I wondered about why Mr and Mrs Smith might have distanced themselves from John when he first came into their care full-time. We talked about the trauma of the separation from his foster mother. Fahlberg (1994) notes the importance of supporting transitions for adopted children, bridging from one placement to another or from foster family to adoptive family, and it was clear that leaving his foster parents must have been severely traumatising for John, but I wondered about how Mr and Mrs Smith felt about it. They said that they, too, had found the experience very traumatic.

Mrs Smith said that she did not feel confident to mother John and by leaving him in a nursery for five days a week she knew that he would be looked after by a highly competent 'surrogate' mother. It became apparent that she had also allowed the school to make decisions about John, decisions that ordinarily would have been made by a child's mother. Both parents said that as John's behaviour became more difficult at home their distancing was a way of coping.

Kirk (1981) writes about how childless couples choosing to adopt can often feel unsure of themselves. He says that this is partly because intrinsic to the nature of adoption is the need to ask someone else for a child. This can leave them questioning their role and ability to parent and also questioning their relationship to the adopted child. Mrs Smith described herself as someone to clothe John rather than to mother him and this seemed to highlight her feelings of inadequacy as a parent and her lack of confidence. Mr and Mrs Smith's defensive response to their feelings was to distance themselves from John, finding 'surrogate' parents for him both in the nursery and also in school. Their lack of availability may have heightened John's challenging behaviours, exacerbating their problems even more.

Music therapy assessment

After the home visit we arranged a music therapy assessment to clarify the reasons for referral and to assess the value of music therapy in helping John with his attachment needs. The assessment was made up of four sessions. The first two sessions were with John alone, although his adoptive mother was observing from within the room. The third session was John with his adoptive father participating fully in the session and the fourth and final session was with John and his adoptive mother participating.

Before detailing the assessment process here is a brief description of the rationale for carrying out music therapy assessment in this way. The music therapy assessment is used to ascertain the suitability of music therapy as an intervention to meet a family's needs, but also to clarify what their needs may be. Children with attachment problems have complex ways of relating and therefore a thorough assessment is vital. I like to see the child alone in order to give me an opportunity to experience them first-hand, to gain a personal experience of being with them. It is interesting to see whether the child can tolerate me placing any structure on our time together or whether their anxiety is so high that they have to control everything. A need to be in control may point to attachment problems, as children who have experienced unresponsive, neglectful parenting find it very difficult to trust that adults know what they want and therefore they feel very unsafe unless they are in control.

Following their individual sessions I like to see the child separately with each parent, as I wish to look at the way each parent interacts with the child and also to see whether the child responds differently to either parent. During the music therapy sessions with the parent and the child together I want to find out the answers to various questions. Can the child choose an instrument for his or her adoptive parent? Can the child accept an instrument chosen for them by their adoptive parent? Can the child share an instrument without needing to control the interaction? Can the child allow the adoptive parent to decide on the rules of a musical game, such as taking turns playing a particular instrument? Does the child look to the adoptive parent for comfort when they are feeling anxious within the session? Does the child show the adoptive parent the instruments they are interested in? The answer to these questions will give me insight into the type of relational problems that a child has.

Initially John presented as a nervous child who seemed uncomfortable engaging with me within the music therapy space. He seemed to reject the greeting song, blocking his ears and turning away. After this John refused to look at or touch any of the instruments. I wondered whether this was an anxious response and I decided to ask Mrs Smith to join in the session. When she came to sit with him John began to show some interest in the musical instruments. He was particularly interested in the metallophone, the cymbal, the reed horn and the ocean drum. For the first 30 minutes of the first assessment session John hid behind the metallophone and the cymbal, hiding his face from me while in his music he was meeting my pulse and engaging in turn-taking exchanges. In this way John's music was interactive, whilst his body language seemed to show that he was unsure whether it was safe to trust me. The volume of John's music also seemed to point to his mixed feelings. His music was either very quiet, almost imperceptible, or very loud. When he played very softly there was sensitivity to his music, whereas when playing very loudly it felt as though he was creating a defensive wall, perhaps to block out his feelings of vulnerability.

Towards the end of the session John came and sat beside me at the piano, carrying the ocean drum. He asked if we could sing a song about the sea while he played the ocean drum. He told me the content of the song and I improvised a simple melody, singing about the sea and the sand. Whilst I sang John swayed the ocean drum in time to the music. When speaking later on to his adoptive mother she said, 'The one time I have seen John be really free was on holiday when we visited the seaside.' It seemed as though John's thematic choice was relevant and it may be that the ocean drum reminded him of this positive experience of the seaside.

When John entered the room for the second session he seemed more confident. He still did not like the opening greeting song, although he giggled when I made it into a joke. He continued to hide behind certain instruments during the session but he also showed the capacity to engage in a more reflective and interactive way. As in the first session, the ocean drum was an instrument that he was particularly drawn to, playing it softly and holding it carefully. He also chose the cymbal again, enjoying both turn-taking with me and also creating a very loud wall of sound, which prevented any interaction at all. Once again John sat beside me at the piano, but this time without any other instrument. He began to play very quietly at the top end of the piano and I supported his playing with a gentle, lilting melody in the Aeolian mode. As he played John hid his face between his arms. Our improvisation ended together. For me this was significant as this shared ending seemed to symbolise negotiation and trust between us. Immediately after this improvisation John left the piano, running into his adoptive mother's arms, kissing and holding her. The session ended shortly afterwards.

When chatting with his adoptive mother after the session she said that she found John's music 'very emotional' and his response to her very unexpected as she was not used to him showing her any spontaneous affection. She said that she did not think that he needed her in this way. It was good to be able to reassure her that my observations from both sessions seemed to show that when John was anxious or feeling vulnerable he needed her and that this was a sign of attachment. This seemed significant as already the music therapy was offering the space for them to relate in a more positive way.

Following a musical interaction John often began to focus on how an instrument was made, becoming quite intellectual, changing the focus from the music and emotion on to the mechanics of the instruments. This happened frequently within each session, although it gradually reduced over the course of the assessment and it was interesting that when his parents were actively involved in a session it happened much less. This seemed important, as when John focused on the mechanics of an instrument he seemed to be exhibiting an intellectual defence to engaging emotionally within the session, also distancing his adoptive parents and myself. A gradual change in this behaviour seemed to point to John's developing trust in the availability of his adoptive parents and security in the therapeutic relationship.

During the assessment session with his adoptive father John created a story. He made little eye contact as he spoke, although his imagination was vivid and his voice was quite unclear. He told a story about a little boy visiting the seaside. Somebody dug a big hole and buried him but then he was rescued. As he ran away, with sticky feet, a car knocked him down. His story seemed to reflect his life experience. Within his birth family John had been neglected and abused, but then he was 'rescued' by his foster family. After 12 months this placement ended as he was moved to his adoptive family. The story seemed to symbolise John's uncertainty that his adoption would continue. Maybe he would be moved on again. John's adoptive father acted out some of the story whilst playing simple, percussive sounds on the guiro. I was able to support their playing from the piano, using short thematic sequences to highlight elements of the story. In this way the story offered the opportunity for John's adoptive father to empathise with him, by taking an active role in the session, whilst also highlighting his availability to his adopted son. John showed warmth and affection for his adoptive father throughout this session.

John entered the therapy room for the final assessment session with a huge smile on his face, announcing that he did not want the 'Hello' or 'Goodbye' songs. It seemed very positive that he could verbalise his feelings and be clear about his desires. However, I wondered if being sung to in this way might have been uncomfortable for him. Also, his rejection of 'Hello' and 'Goodbye' songs may have pointed to his inability, at this stage of the work, to work through past attachment and loss experiences, something that is a large part of adoption.

The session continued with John enthusiastically choosing a buffalo drum for his mother to play whilst he chose the reed horn. Their music was loud and energetic. I took my clarinet, improvising a bright melody in C major, and we marched playfully around the room. John seemed much more confident throughout this session, not needing to hide at all.

During an improvisation in which John played the recorder and his mother played the tambourine, John told a story about a train. Again, John seemed to use his story to process difficult events and feelings, allowing for empathy and understanding from his adoptive mother. The story had background music throughout and, after a particularly engaging improvisation in which we ended together, John seemed embarrassed, smiling at me and putting his head down. It seemed as though musical connectedness and interaction was becoming a little more bearable as he did not need to talk about the mechanics of the instruments to block out his feelings. It was also clear from this session that his adoptive mother was intuitively responding to John's music. She affirmed him throughout.

After the assessment sessions both Mr and Mrs Smith said that they felt uncomfortable at hearing John's stories. This seemed to be a totally understandable response, as adults want to believe that children are happy and not experiencing problems. However, the stories that John told in his therapy sessions must have been meaningful for him as he repeated them word for word to the absent parent on both occasions. It is possible that in telling these stories in the third person, John could distance himself from them and process his negative experiences more effectively than if he was talking in the first person. It was safe for him to engage in this way. It also offered the opportunity, within a secure space, to arouse empathy and understanding from his adoptive parents, as they shared in the story. I was concerned that John be enabled to share in this way and for it to be accepted and valued, as failure to do so may undermine his already vulnerable self-esteem.

Over the course of the assessment there were some distinct changes in John's behaviour. He began to make more direct eye contact as the sessions progressed and he engaged more fully in the music as the assessment went on, retreating less into an intellectual defence. John began to reflect on and process difficult experiences and feelings through story-telling, and in free improvisation, and when he spoke his voice became clearer and more confident.

The assessment sessions seemed to show that music therapy had the potential to help the family in various ways.

- It could offer them time to work on their relationships and to provide a more positive way of relating. In making the sessions flexible in their timing it may be possible for both Mr and Mrs Smith to be involved in the work.

- The assessment showed that music therapy had the potential to provide a safe space for John to explore his feelings, to develop understanding of emotions both in himself and in others.

- Involving his adoptive parents in the work, seeing them as part of the healing process, enabled them to become more empathic in their responses to him, and also offered them emotional support and empathy. It was hoped that through this process they might become more confident in their approach to John.

- By committing themselves to attending weekly music therapy sessions, John's adoptive parents would be making a positive effort to re-engage with him.

Following a break for Christmas and securing funding for the work to take place, weekly sessions of music therapy began in the January, two months later. The work lasted for seven months.

Weekly music therapy

For the first eight sessions of therapy John would hide at the beginning of each session. When this was challenged he would say, 'But I need to hide'. He needed to be found by either his mother or his father before he could engage in the music therapy session. It was almost as though he was checking out their absence and return, their availability to him. Occasionally John would hide during a session. When asked why he might need to do this, his response was always associated with needing to protect himself from some danger such as someone entering the therapy room or something hurting him. If John ever heard a noise outside the therapy room, or he thought that someone might come in, he would literally freeze and be unable to continue playing the instruments until he was reassured. I wondered if this and the hiding might have been an unconscious association with abuse as a very young child, as this was not ruled out by social services when he was initially taken into care. Mrs Smith found this particularly interesting as she said he sometimes hid at home and she and her husband found it frustrating. They had never before considered why John might be doing this. Sinason (1992, p.186) says that a safe-enough attachment is a prerequisite to play. When he felt safe enough and secure enough John no longer needed to hide, either at the beginning of the sessions or during them.

During the first five sessions of therapy John told us that there was a boy hiding in the metallophone. When he was asked about him John said that the boy was hiding and he did not want to see anyone. At one point John said the boy was hiding from me, the therapist. Whilst the boy was hiding inside the instrument John asked his mother and me to pump air, with him, into the metallophone, using swanny whistles. This seemed interesting as John suffers with asthma and needs an inhaler on occasion. Once again it seemed like John's playing was showing his mother and me how to care for him. At the beginning of the sixth session John announced that the little boy had come out. Soon after this John stopped hiding, both in therapy and also at home.

When John first returned to music therapy, following the break after the assessment, he resisted improvising. However, he did use the instruments to play, as with the swanny whistles, but not to make music. This was interesting, as playing in this way seemed to be the means by which he could become safe. Pavlicevic (1997, p.143) says, 'One of the main functions of the therapeutic space is to enable the client to feel safe enough within it to risk feeling unsafe'. John needed to feel safe enough before he could once again engage in free improvisation, to allow himself to be vulnerable in the music.

It was through using the instruments that John seemed to develop his play skills. His adoptive parents had described how at home he played alone and it was difficult to engage with him. Music was the perfect medium through which he could learn to share, to take turns, to be with others in a safe, contained space. John began by asking if we could play some party games, such as musical chairs or musical statues. John, his adoptive mother and myself took it in turns to start and stop the music from the piano. Gradually, John's need to control subsided and he could trust us, the adults, to take charge. These games developed into rolling the ocean drum to and from one another as we sat in a circle, or taking turns beating on a drum. Mr and Mrs Smith said that they had never played with John in this way. Again, this was interesting because playing in this way became something they then did at home, with John's toys. His social worker noticed a distinct change when she visited the family at home because John engaged her in playing a game.

When John did improvise again he was particularly drawn to the reed horn, the cymbal and the drums. Mrs Smith was concerned that his music was too loud. I considered with her whether his loud music was a way of protecting himself, and suggested that maybe if she met the volume of his music as a way of empathising with his feelings, he might not need to play so loudly. John chose to play the standing cymbal, giving his adoptive mother two beaters to play with him. I moved to the piano, to support and contain their playing. They took it in turns to play the cymbal. John's playing was very loud and initially Mrs Smith winced at the volume. I encouraged her to meet his music and tentatively she began to play. Eventually Mrs Smith met the volume of John's playing. John thought this was great fun and they laughed together. I suggested that their music sounded rather like children splashing in water in their wellington boots on a rainy day. It was playful and engaging, and I supported their music from the piano with loud cluster chords. We all ended together. This seemed significant as it showed unity and trust in negotiating the ending of the music. Following this improvisation John did not seem to need to play the cymbal so loudly in future sessions. He had been heard and responded to effectively by his adoptive mother.

During earlier sessions of music therapy John's music therapy sessions could be described as manic. His music was often loud and fast, and he would run around. As the sessions progressed so John's music became more reflective, calmer, leaving more space to think. Rather like the cymbal creating a protective barrier, his loud music prevented thinking about bad experiences. Bion (1962, pp.110–120) says that in order to process a thought one has to think and that, sometimes, when trauma has been experienced, thinking can be felt as a painful sensation. As John felt safer so his music calmed and he left more space to reflect. This was highlighted in his ability to answer questions about how he might be feeling and to verbalise thoughts and feelings without being prompted to do so. His parents noted that at home his violent outbursts had reduced considerably and he had begun to tell them when he was upset.

John used his playing in music therapy to work through events that may be potentially traumatic. Twelve weeks into the work there was to be break for a holiday. Owing to John's experiences of attachment and loss as an adopted child it was important to think about this break and allow time for it to be processed. I mentioned the break to John three weeks in advance and he used this time to prepare himself. John built a boat with the base of the metallophone and into the boat he placed all the instruments and a toy penguin that he had brought to therapy. With the help of his adoptive father and myself, John acted out a story of the penguin going on holiday to an island (created from the cymbal head) in the boat, catching some fish and then returning home. He acted out this story twice during the course of the session. He then asked me to keep something, which I had to bring back to his next music therapy session. He seemed to be making sure that I would not forget him whilst we were apart and I said as much to him, reassuring him that I would be thinking of him during the break.

Mid-way through the work John had to be admitted into hospital for a minor ear operation. When he came into the music therapy room, on the day before he went into hospital, he was absolutely silent and completely motionless. His mother offered him the ocean drum to play and he sat with it in his arms without making a single sound, something that is very difficult to do with an ocean drum. This experience of John gave me an insight into how he may have been when he left his foster mother to be with Mr and Mrs Smith, unable to engage with anyone, emotionally shut down. It was possible that the impending hospital visit may have been reminding him of previous times when he had been left alone in hospital. His mother and I decided to use the session as a time to reflect on what may be worrying him and to offer John reassurance about her availability on the day. As it happened John managed the situation well and came back to music therapy the following week ready to play. Mrs Smith and I then had the opportunity to discuss the playing together. Gradually she was growing in confidence and insight towards him.

In the final weeks of the work John showed freedom in his improvisations. He enjoyed surrounding himself with lots of instruments and creating colourful soundscapes. The music seemed to pour out of him, as he enjoyed the freedom that the therapy gave him.

Conclusion

As the case study has highlighted, over the course of the work John's anxieties reduced and he was able to begin trusting his adoptive parents. The music gave them a medium through which this could take place, as they engaged interactively with one another for the first time. In responding to John's music Mr and Mrs Smith found his innate language and they began to communicate effectively with him. In this way, rather like a mother responding to the early sounds of her baby's babbling, the interactive music making became foundational to the development of their relationship with their adopted son.

As Mr and Mrs Smith grew more confident in their ability to play musically with John, so they became more responsive to his needs at home and their faith in their ability to parent him grew. Previously, as mentioned earlier, Mr and Mrs Smith had distanced themselves from their adopted son both physically and emotionally and they interpreted his more challenging behaviours as 'naughtiness', finding it difficult to understand why he might be acting in particular ways. Their approach towards him may well have heightened his attachment behaviours, which therefore created more and more tension in the family. If John had received music therapy alone, without the involvement of his parents, then in many ways this could have distanced them further from their adopted son, contributing to their feelings of inadequacy by leaving a 'professional' to solve the problem.

Music therapy gave them time with John and in so doing the negative patterns of relating that they had been used to as a family could be broken. Studies into late-placed adoptions show that the most effective outcomes occur when parents are prepared to dedicate both time and energy to their adopted child. Mr and Mrs Smith's commitment to the work showed John that they were willing to commit to him long term. They were available and responsive to him.

Engaging the whole family in music therapy meant that they learnt to play with one another. These very practical play skills are vital for children, as it is through play that they learn to negotiate, build trust in others and learn about themselves in relation to other people. Working in this way gave John the possibility to build trust in his adoptive parents, whilst creating space for him to reflect on his past and present experiences. He was able to use the music to explore some difficult emotions without the fear of rejection. The sessions also enabled containment for the whole family unit. By individually listening to and valuing their feelings, Mr and Mrs Smith became the catalyst for healing in John's life and music therapy the medium through which this could take place.

This case highlights the value and importance of involving adoptive parents in music therapy when their child is presenting with attachment difficulties. John developed trust in his adoptive parents through the art of making music together. It is almost as though their creative musical output represented the positive process towards a healthier way of relating as a family. Before music therapy Mr and Mrs Smith had distanced themselves from their adopted son, finding surrogate parents for him in nursery and school. They had little confidence in their ability to parent him. Interacting musically with John developed their confidence as parents and this piece of work was vital as they were able to take responsibility for his needs, providing both emotional and physical containment.

Chapter 9

A Piece of the Puzzle
Music Therapy with Looked-after Teenagers and their Carers

Joy Hasler

Celebrate Vicki!
Not scared or frightened any more
Happy being me because I'm so lovely
Celebrate Vicki happy and free
Celebrate Vicki's life, *come on!* (A verse of a song by Vicki, age 16)

Introduction

Each local authority provides services for children and young people in their care in the form of a regulated and complex system designed to protect the needs of the most vulnerable children in society. Young people who cannot live with their birth family, for whatever reason, collect around them a team who have the responsibility for making decisions as substitute parents on behalf of the child. If therapy is required the therapist becomes a part of this care team, a piece in the puzzle, with a role that is complementary to the roles and responsibilities of the other people in the team.

This chapter presents a model for music therapy with looked-after teenagers that includes their carers. It begins by drawing a map of the people around a teenager in care followed by the key issues which affect them and all those who live and work with them. A personal account is given of the development of a therapeutic model, based on stages of trauma recovery, with a focus on the attachment relationship between the teenagers and their carers. Carers are considered part of the therapeutic team and are invited to take part in the sessions. The chapter is illustrated with examples from sessions at different stages of therapy.

Corporate care

In March 2006 there were 60,300 children and young people in care in the UK, 70 per cent of whom were in foster care. Some 8100 young people aged 16 or over left care during 2005–2006. In the same year 23,000 children and young people had been in care for two and a half years or more (DfES 2006). These figures reveal the significant numbers of teenagers for whom residential or foster care is their home. Some will be approaching independence, many will have been in care for several years and many will have had several moves; most will have experienced significant trauma and all will have suffered separation from important people in their lives. Many will need therapeutic support either in the short term to help with specific difficulties or in the longer term as they struggle to overcome the effects of early life neglect, rejection or abuse.

The music therapist working with a young person in care enters a world of policies, regulations and finite resources. Being part of a looked-after young person's care team requires a mental map representing the roles, responsibilities and protocols, a map that will be different in each case. There can be several key people in the life of a young person (see Figure 9.1). Some have essential roles, such as the social worker and teacher, but others are included as needs are identified or circumstances dictate. The young people themselves are respected as key people in their own life planning. A music therapist can be contracted by any one of the agencies involved but will need to appreciate the roles and responsibilities of all the key people.

It is common for people working or living with a looked-after teenager each to have very different perceptions of that person. Difficulties can arise when each worker or carer has their own perception and together they are trying to reach an agreement about the needs of that young person. For the music therapist coming into the team this can cause confusion and a fragmented picture. The answers to the following questions could help the music therapist to develop an integrated picture of the young person and a map of the key people involved.

- Who are the people responsible for decision-making in any area of the young person's life?
- What is the history of the young person?

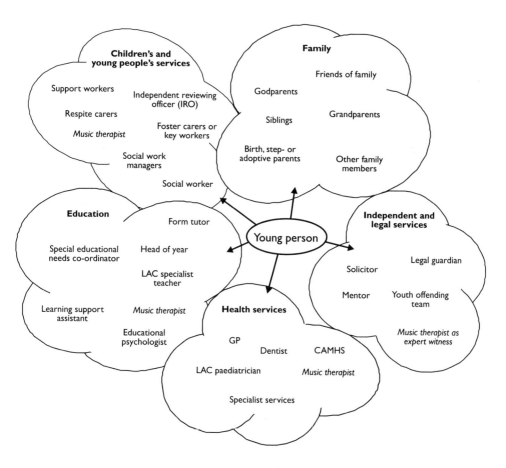

Figure 9.1 Key people in the life of a looked-after young person

- Who is currently doing work with the young person and with what aims?
- Has there been any therapeutic work in the past – and where are the reports?
- Who is included in the confidential circle of the young person?
- What are the expectations of music therapy by the agency, the carers and the young person?

The last question, regarding expectations, does not have clear or straightforward answers. It is not easy to identify expectations when the young person's behaviour may seem to be at odds with what they have asked for when they say something to one person and the opposite to someone else. However, clarity of purpose can emerge when expectations are clear between all the key people involved.

Key issues for looked-after young people and their carers

Bereavement, trauma and attachment are key issues for young people in care and, as a result, secondary trauma is an issue for those around them. These factors are inter-related, as the young person will have experienced separation from family members, who may also be the source of neglect or abuse, and everyone concerned with the young person will be collectively and personally affected in different ways according to their own experiences of bereavement or trauma.

Bereavement is significant for looked-after young people, as all of them will have been separated for short or long periods from their families of origin, and many will have had several moves during their time in care, but bereavement is more than the loss of loved ones. It can also be about the loss of culture, community, familiar places, hopes for the future and a feeling of belonging to a family; important factors which offered familiarity and security even when the circumstances were perceived by others to be unsafe. The loss of any, or a combination, of these factors can be traumatic, and looked-after young people may feel they have lost everything.

Music therapy in the field of bereavement is well documented by therapists working in private practice, hospitals, hospices and care centres (Aldridge 2004; Bright 1994; Pavlicevic 2005). Music therapy has been shown to assist bereaved people cope with grief, loss, pain, anxiety and a feeling of hopelessness, and it brings relief. Shared improvisation of music gives expression to deep feelings and brings them into a form that can then be discussed (Aldridge 2004).

Trauma is defined as the overwhelming experience of pain or anxiety (shock) with a response of fear, helplessness or horror (Briere 1992; Cairns 2002; Sutton 2002). Trauma may be caused by a sudden or serious incident or by an environment of high stress and fear resulting from neglect or repeated separation from the attachment figure. The overwhelming aspects of trauma affect the whole person (Schore 2003; Sutton 2002). Early traumatic experiences cause the child to develop protective behaviours for survival, based on the instinctive responses of fight, flight and freeze. In fight mode the young person may become aggressive; in flight mode they will be hypervigilant; and in freeze mode they may appear switched off or dissociated from their surroundings.

When a young person is placed in a loving home with caring people the antisocial aspects of their protective behaviours become a source of stress, and the result is often a system of rewards and sanctions in an attempt to change these behaviours. But this does not address the message the young person is attempting to convey: that he does not feel safe and does not trust the adults around him to keep him safe, and that 'unsafe', in his experience, can be perceived as life-threatening. The traumatised young person is not going to let go of his protective system easily.

Trauma causes splits between mind and body, fragmentation and wholeness, chaos and order, and hopelessness and hope. Musical improvisation, shared with a therapist in a safe place, offers a healing bridge and can allow these elements to be expressed, explored and balanced. This process creates a deep reciprocal relationship which enables healing and transformation (Aldridge 2004; Pavlicevic 2002).

Attachment is the behaviour infants use to alert their parents to the fact that they have needs which require attention or that they feel anxious, unsafe or hurt (Howe 2005; Prior and Glaser 2006). This provokes a reaction in the parent that satisfies both the child and the parent, with the magical micro-moment of connection at the time of anticipated resolution of need being called 'attunement' (Stern 1987), a term with musical connotations. The moment of attunement is the space in which the infant's affect is regulated and he develops trust that his needs will be met. When the child's needs are met, the parent and child can enjoy each other's company in the security of a strong bond. A mother has as much need to be able to satisfy her infant as the infant has to have his needs met. When this reciprocal system is negative or breaks down, the child develops defensive behaviour patterns that enable him to survive the resulting trauma of his needs not being met. The infant is still compelled to make an attachment, but the pattern is negative and insecure or lacks any organisation.

As the developmental stage of teenagers is naturally to move towards independence, it may seem incongruous to focus on attachment patterns. The young person's unmet infancy needs collide with their developing identity needs, creating confusion and internal conflict. Positive attachment patterns are, if still insecure, crucial for the development of a secure base from which to move to independence with a positive sense of self and confidence in sustaining long-term relationships. Music offers teenagers an age-appropriate medium to replay and reform early attachment patterns, especially when shared with the attachment figure in their life.

Secondary trauma

The reciprocal element of attachment, the devastating nature of trauma and the relational aspects of bereavement cause anyone who becomes attuned to a traumatised young person also to be affected by, and vulnerable to, the impact of the trauma. This is secondary trauma (Cairns 1999; Figley 2002), in which a connection is made between the young person's traumatic experience, the carer or professional's own traumatic memory and their need to work in the field of care. The effect on music therapists of working with trauma victims has been recognised and documented (Sutton 2002) as calling for self-care as if they are 'instruments requiring fine tuning' (Austin 2002, p.241).

If secondary trauma is recognised and addressed by the care team of a looked-after teenager, the team will want to work in an integrated way, supporting each other, responding to challenges with cohesion and seeking to represent the whole picture of the young person in context. If not, the picture becomes separated and broken, representing the fragmentation of the traumatised young person. When carers are part of a fragmented team the additional stress can be overwhelming. They can feel deskilled, frustrated and blamed for the difficulties in the placement. This then has an effect on the young person who will pick up the lack of confidence and feel insecure as a result, as can be seen in the following example from a session near the beginning of a short-term music therapy programme.

Steve and his carers, Janet and Dave
'YOU'RE USELESS AT THAT'

Steve mocked Janet: 'You're useless at that – you don't even know how to hold it properly.' Steve smiled at Dave as they played their drums together. Janet put her instrument down and turned away. Later, she told me that she had wanted to walk out of the room.

The setting is a room in a creative arts therapy centre, with a range of percussion instruments, guitars and a piano. The seating is set like a family lounge with a settee and low soft chairs. Steve is 13 and comes to therapy because his carers are exhausted with trying to manage his behaviour. We are playing a game of follow-the-leader and at this point Dave is the leader.

When the game stopped I asked Steve 'What do you think Janet is feeling when you tell her she is useless?' After a couple of 'I dunno's, he said he thought Janet would be upset. 'Has something happened for you to want Janet to feel upset, Steve?' He muttered 'She wouldn't let me talk to Mum on the phone.' Janet agreed and said it had become a heated argument.

The decision that Steve could only speak to his mother by prior arrangement was not made by his carers but collectively by the care team who felt that contact needed monitoring.

I suggested that we could replay the argument using music instead of voices. I asked them all to choose instruments to represent how they felt before and then during the argument. They became engaged in trying and choosing instruments with different qualities. They searched for the right degree of energy for the argument and began to laugh at their attempts. The discussion as they explored the sounds led to a conversation about Steve's feelings for his mother. Janet said, 'I know you love your mother and that not being able to speak to her must make you very sad.' Steve turned away from Janet pulling his collar up round his face. I waited for a moment, holding the silence, then gently suggested to Janet and Dave that we play some music to reflect the feelings we were seeing. Following my lead, they chose melodic instruments with mellow sounds. The music had a clear regular beat with slow, soft melodies that both clashed and harmonised. Through our music we attempted to connect with the feeling of sadness that Steve was showing, without being intrusive. There was no move from Janet to comfort him or from Dave to try to jolly him out of it, but an acceptance of the painful place he was in. After a while Steve turned, picked up a beater and joined in the music. The mood changed and became light-hearted and fun. The ending came with a crescendo, a crash from Steve on the cymbal and laughter from everyone.

Becoming attuned to the anxiety of a young person can be painful for the carers but can also give the message to the young person that their needs are recognised and understood. Offering physical comfort can be unwelcome, but making connections through the music can provide comfort at a distance that can feel safe.

When the young person targets one parent rather than both, this can cause splitting: playing people off against each other, causing conflict in their relationships. This is a common symptom among adoptive parents and carers of traumatised children (Hirst 2005) with potentially devastating effect. Support for carers from someone who understands these dynamics must be available alongside music therapy. In a later conversation with Dave and Janet we discussed the effect that splitting had on their relationship and considered what they could do to look after themselves.

A personal journey

Frustration at not getting the help I needed for the looked-after children who were part of our family led me to the idea of becoming a music therapist. From the combined experience of over 20 years as a foster carer, an adoptive parent and voluntary work as a co-ordinator for Adoption UK (then called Parent to Parent Information on Adoption Service (PPIAS)), I gained an insight into the care systems for children and young people. I had experienced the search for therapeutic help and the battles for funding, and knew that the resources required were limited and hard to access. As a music teacher in a special school I could see the potential of music as a means of healing relationships.

I retrained as a music therapist with the specific aim of working in this field, initially setting up in private practice. Excluding adoptive parents and carers from the therapy session of the young people began to seem inconsistent with the aims of therapy and the young people's needs for positive attachment relationships. I wanted to find out if the capacity of music therapy to transform relationships could be used to enhance the attachment relationship between the young person and their carer. I had shared the carers' experiences of managing complicated contact arrangements or coping with disturbed nights or the destruction of anything positive. I believed that the difficulties they were experiencing could be explored through music, but realised that working in this way would require some careful considerations and further training.

My journey included training with the Post-Adoption Centre in London, the British Agency for Adoption and Fostering (BAAF), the UK Society for the Study of Dissociation (UKSSD) and the Association for Treatment and Training in the Attachment of Children (ATTACh). After a few years building up knowledge of the field and experience in private practice, I was joined by three other creative arts therapists and a special needs teacher, and together, in 2001, we set up a company to offer a specialist service, called Creative Attachment Therapy for CHildren in foster and adoptive families (CATCH-point).

CATCH-point

The aim at CATCH-point is to develop an integrated approach to therapeutic support for the family whilst focusing on the attachment relationship: that of the young person and caregiver.

When a teenager is referred to CATCH-point, their carers or key workers are usually concerned about the young person's behaviour, either at home or at school, or both. The young person will have agreed to come to therapy but may have very different expectations from their carers about what is achievable. Many come with the assumption that it is going to be another means of controlling them and their behaviours, and most arrive with suspicion and anxiety. Carers often come with hopes of a complete change so that they can develop closeness, fun and a sense of belonging with the young person in their care. The referring agencies have very different expectations according to their experience of creative arts therapies. Their concern is to get the best service in the interests of the young person and trying an unfamiliar therapy, such as music therapy, requires trust.

Although direct work with young people may be identified as needed, it is rare in a sparsely resourced system and when it happens the focus is usually on 'changing behaviour performance...with very little attention to questions of motivation and need' (Biehal 2005, p.131). At CATCH-point the focus is moved away from 'changing behaviours' to making connections between the feelings and needs which cause the behaviours. The young people can then be helped to make choices that are not governed by their distrust of adults, but by a growing resilience and security. For some teenagers this is a long process and for others a short programme starts a process that can be continued at home. In the following example from a session after about six months of music therapy, an unexpected reaction led to the carers being able to help the young person make a connection between her extreme anxiety and her need for security of placement.

Stella and her carers, Jill and Chris
'DON'T SHOUT AT ME'

Six months after starting therapy, Stella arrived for her session, bright and enthusiastic, with her carers, Jill and Chris. Within less than a minute Stella's manner had changed. She sat slumped, looking down at the floor muttering that she didn't want to talk about anything and she didn't see why she had to come. I looked at the carers and they shrugged indicating that they didn't know the cause.

Stella is 14 years old with moderate learning difficulties and has had many moves before coming to live with Jill and Chris nearly two years previously.

I asked Stella to choose instruments for everyone, which she did slowly without enthusiasm. The carers and I started to play together, trying to reflect the mood we were witnessing. Stella sat silently with her head down. Suddenly she crashed the cymbal repeatedly. It seemed as though she couldn't make a big enough sound to express what she wanted to say. Jill and Chris and I stopped and let her play a solo of crashing chaos.

After a while Stella started to laugh and then stopped. 'Did you like that?' she asked. I wanted to show acceptance without giving an opinion of her music. I replied 'I'd like us to join in with you. Which instruments would you like us to play, Stella?' She carefully chose clanging sounds whilst laughing in a mocking way, indicating that she was looking for sounds her carers would not like. From the carers' expressions I picked up some resistance to playing these jangling sounds, but I hoped that the trust that we had built over the last few months would enable them to follow my lead and play the instruments Stella was choosing for them, accepting the quality of sound she wanted.

The 'together' music shook the house and we couldn't sustain it for long because it was too loud, but we didn't need to. Stella curled up on her chair with her jacket pulled up round her face. She seemed alone and unable to ask for comfort; unable to find the words to say what she was feeling; unable to make sense of the powerful emotion that had come to the surface. She got up and left the room. I was not worried about safety as I knew there were other people around but I was concerned that she wanted to isolate herself when she was distressed. I went to the door and found her in the corridor. 'Don't shout at me,' she said. I agreed that no one should be shouted at and then invited her to return when she felt ready. I returned to the room, leaving the door slightly open, to play music with a regular beat, with Jill and Chris on xylophones, small drums and a guitar. Stella returned and sat for a while then picked up a beater and joined in with us, but this time matching the mood and energy of the music we were playing.

During the session I make choices about how I respond to the music of the young person. If the music is chaotic I may choose to join in and encourage carers to do the same but if it is near the end of a session I may choose to regulate and organise the energy by responding with a soft beat, which can help in the same way as the regulating effect of a mother tapping the back of her distressed infant. Finding the balance between shared music-making and solo improvisation is a matter of making intuitive responses, and in this session we let Stella play her crashing music without accompanying her. Solo playing enables the young person to have individual expression and to feel heard and appreciated, whereas shared playing encourages co-operation and connection. Either or both are acceptable giving everyone some choice about how much they participate.

Balancing discussion and music enables connections to be processed. In discussion after the music, we discovered that Stella was worried about the near anniversary of moving in with Jill and Chris, knowing that she had never been in a placement for longer than two years. The approaching date had become a trigger to past trauma; a recurring nightmare of moving, goodbyes, lost friends, lost treasures and living with strangers. Stella was finding it impossible to talk about this, but in the session had managed to convey her fear that she might lose the people she loved and who loved her. The words 'Don't shout at me' (no one had shouted) indicated that past memories of times when she had been shouted at had been triggered. After Stella had shared these feelings with her carers through their music, she was able to put them into words, and the discussion moved on to how they could celebrate the anniversary.

CATCH-point therapeutic model

The therapeutic model used at CATCH-point is based on the following assumptions.

- All young people in care will have suffered significant losses and may have difficulties with attachment, self-regulation and social interactions.

- Antisocial behaviours carry important messages about how the young person is feeling and need to be recognised.

- Trauma experienced by the young person will affect those who care for or work with them as secondary trauma.

- Carers should be considered part of the healing team.

These assumptions inform all aspects of the support services of which there are four strands. Creative arts therapy including music therapy is one strand. The other three are concerned with support for the carers. These are as follows.

- Developing a common understanding of the long-term effect of early trauma and insecure attachment patterns.
- Giving guidance on understanding and managing challenging behaviour.
- Helping carers to recognise and relieve stress.

If these strands are not offered by other supporting agencies then CATCH-point includes them in the therapeutic programme, involving a different member of the team.

Role of carers in therapy

Before any therapy starts the music therapist meets with the carers and social worker to discuss what is happening in the placement, what they hope can be achieved, how we operate, their role in therapy and what additional support they need. Together, we agree goals for therapy and a time for review. The carers are respected as the authorities in their home, but are asked to let the therapist be in charge of the session, setting boundaries and directing activities as appropriate. It is important that there is one person who facilitates the session to avoid confusion. Carers are informed of the process of therapy so that they can feel confident in what they are being asked to do. This confidence is important to empower them, and not to undermine their authority. CATCH-point seeks to work in partnership with carers, and telephone conversations between sessions offer time to sort out any misunderstandings and to elicit feedback.

Therapeutic approach

The music therapy sessions have a balance between shared playing and individual playing, between playing music and dialogue, and between raising and regulating anxiety levels. It is important that a young person can use the space to express extreme emotional states if they choose, but also that they leave the session in a state of low anxiety and safety. The therapist tries to raise anxiety levels gently through creative challenges, such as asking the young person to take a lead, and then ending the session in a calm place by lowering the energy levels in the music. Howe (2005) cites Cozolino as recommending 'controlled exposure to stress during therapy as a way in which therapists have attempted to harness the interaction of stress and learning to change the brain in a manner promoting mental health' (Cozolino 2002, p.24). Negative behaviours may be evoked when stress is increased and then alternative responses can be explored. Exploring raised anxiety through improvised music is like the suspense of discordance, which resolves in harmony or the suspense of infants' unmet needs which resolve in reciprocal attunement. Learning to anticipate resolution helps to develop the young person's ability to regulate their own stress levels.

The therapeutic model used at CATCH-point is based on trauma recovery models of Brown, Scheflin and Hammond (1998), Fosha (2003) and James (1996), which follow a similar path from the presenting state of disorder through to the desired state of integration, openness, trust and relatedness to others (see Table 9.1).

Each stage of recovery requires a different approach. We will look at the first stage of disorder or defence later. In the stage of stabilisation or reorder the therapist uses structured activities and is mainly directive with the aim of building security in the placement. The music is organised into games and structured activities to encourage respect for boundaries, reciprocal interaction and shared appreciation. Within these games there will be spaces for free expression in preparation for the next stage.

The stage of integration or reframing moves to more unstructured activities with a non-directive approach, for free improvisation and shared emotional expression. The focus is on making sense of feelings, experiences and behaviours. This is achieved through curiosity and exploration both verbally and musically. The carers join in the improvisations or receive them as listeners as they wish.

The stages are not worked through neatly from start to finish, and the stage of disorder, which is usually the presenting stage, is often revisited, giving everyone a feeling of 'stuckness'. Although this is described as an aspect of the first stage, it is the experience of staff at CATCH-point that it is also a reviewing stage. As the therapy becomes challenging, anxiety is raised and the young person retries old methods of protection (antisocial behaviours) only to discover that they are no longer as effective. This can cause a state of panic and anxiety because the young person feels vulnerable and unsafe, but it is not the same state that they were in when they started therapy and appears to be a vital part of recovery. The feeling of 'stuckness' can be a reminder of the therapeutic journey, leading to a review and rethinking exercise. Is the pace right? Should we return to structured activities? Are there changes in the young person's life that are creating raised anxiety? Do we need to find out more information? Sometimes it is just a question of

Table 9.1 Comparison of trauma recovery models

Brown, Scheflin and Hammond (1998)	James (1996)	Fosha (2003)	CATCH-point	Description
		Defence	Disorder	Stuck/superficial/ Challenging/resistant/protected Defences against relatedness
Stabilisation	Communication	Transitional affects	Re-order	Identify feelings in self and others Establishing boundaries Explore new ways of expressing feelings Sharing creative activities
	Sorting out	Core affects	Reframe	Make sense of experiences and feelings Looking to carers for comfort and guidance
Integration	Education	Transformational affects		Processing the trauma Affect regulation Rebuilding cognitive constructs
Adaptation	Perspective	Core state	Reconnection	Developing a positive sense of self, well-being, relational experiences of closeness and openness Able to process shame and repair Re-establishing social and emotional connectedness

giving the young person time and space to rest until they are ready to take the next step forward. The music therapist and carers try to accompany the young person with acceptance, tolerating their fragmentation and exploring each of the pieces as they grow together (Pavlicevic 2002). This is the stage of greatest vulnerability as it can be the point where some carers give up and a young person moves on to a new placement. Therefore, anticipating this stage from the beginning can be helpful.

The last stage of adaptation or reconnectedness is one that mainly happens away from the therapy space when the young person puts into practice skills of negotiation and repair that enable them to resolve difficulties and develop a positive sense of self. The music therapy sessions become a celebration of progress.

The following example is an overview of the process through nine months of therapy. By the end of the programme the young person was able to ask her carer to help her so that they could sort out difficulties together.

Emma and her carer, Jane
'NOW IT HURTS'

Emma came to therapy with enthusiasm. She knew what she wanted to do and what she hoped to achieve. She wanted to write songs and sing them. She was focused and clear and knew what she wanted to sing about: her feelings of sadness at the many people she had lost and her struggles with friendships at school. But she also wanted to write and sing songs about the things she was proud of. Together with Jane, we wrote the words down and decided which instruments she wanted for accompaniment.

When she came to therapy, Emma was 13 years old and had lived with Jane, a single carer, for three years. Her 18-year-old brother, with whom she had regular contact, had recently moved back in with their mother. This was causing Emma confusion and anxiety as living at home was not an option for her so she felt excluded from the relationship that her brother and her mother were building.

At a very young age, Emma learnt that stealing gives you a buzz that takes away the pain of sad feelings, so she became good at it and proud of her stealing abilities. Not only did it help to confirm her belief in herself that she was 'bad', but it got her a lot of negative attention. Jane had tried many recommended strategies to get Emma to stop and was beginning to feel that she would not be able to keep her for much longer. This provoked a fear of rejection, and Emma was, in turn, rejecting Jane in preparation for what she felt was the inevitable. They were stuck and couldn't see a way forward, but they were prepared to try something new, and music therapy was welcomed as a last chance to keep them together.

Emma and Jane hugged, cried, laughed, argued, sang and banged their way through sessions. Jane said she felt as if she was 'unravelling', and that the music therapy sessions helped her to feel that they were connected again.

The session was divided into part music playing and part discussion. Sometimes the conversation was about the next song that Emma wanted to sing and sometimes it was about difficulties in their home. Emma and Jane both realised that when they were angry they could not think sensibly so together they worked out some symbols and actions, such as putting a frog instrument on the mantelpiece when either felt sad or in need of a hug. They also developed a code for letting each other know when they needed some space.

Together we explored the feelings that Emma was afraid of. Through the music and discussion the feelings were shared and became safe. Emma worked out for herself that stealing was her protection against her inner pain, so she decided to stop. In a session near the end of our programme, Emma said 'I've given up stealing and now it hurts – so what have you got to put in its place?'

This is a question that has stayed with me. If I am asking young people to let go of a protective behaviour, what is on offer to put in its place? The answer must come from a reciprocal relationship of mutual respect, security and comfort, but unless the carers are moving in the same direction as the young person in terms of understanding the behaviours this is unlikely to happen. For Emma to trust Jane to comfort her and keep her safe was hard, but the affection that had grown between them through the music helped Emma to realise that this is what they were working towards. Young people who have been let down repeatedly or have been rejected need to be very brave to dare to trust again and Emma was no different. The dynamics of the relationship that forms through music-making challenges the young person's lack of trust in caregivers, and this can bring about panic and a state of 'stuckness'. The young person may not feel ready to embrace such a relationship and so they hide behind protective behaviours. This was a place Emma and Jane revisited several times, but each time recovered to move on to celebrate achievements.

Contact is a common factor in the lives of young people in care that often requires interventions from social workers, so Emma, Jane and I met with her social worker at home, and together they were able to work out a plan for contact with Emma's mother that would protect her from more involvement than she could manage without losing contact with her brother. Emma and Jane both wanted me to be present at this meeting as they wanted my support.

Conclusion

The young people who have been described in this chapter have shown that through shared creativity their relationship with their carers can be transformed. They came to music therapy with distrust and it required considerable bravery to open themselves to a process of reconnection to their feelings and traumatic memories. Each one brought something different that they could share with the therapist and their carers. A model of music therapy that includes the carers provides a framework from which feelings and responses can be explored, offering choices that were previously inaccessible. To work in this way a music therapist needs to appreciate the effect on themselves of being part of a care team of which they are important but also only one piece in the puzzle that makes up the whole picture.

Chapter 10

Living with Dying
Reflections on Family Music Therapy with Children near the End of Life

Claire Flower

Introduction

Music therapists have, for many years, worked with children who have profound and multiple disabilities, including those with complex medical needs. In more recent years, however, therapists have found a place working with children who may not be expected to live into adulthood. This has largely come about because of the development of the children's hospice movement within the UK.

This chapter tells the stories of music therapy with three such children and their families as these children reached the end of their lives. These stories are based in part on clinical observations and descriptions of the time spent with these girls and each family. The families have also been generous in talking with me subsequently about their experience of music therapy. The inclusion of some of their thoughts makes this chapter a testimony to the characters and lives of their three children.

Although all of these families have lived through the death of a child, each family's situation and their use of music therapy have differed greatly. These differences, as well as the similarities, contribute towards our understanding of clinical work with people facing such life-shattering events. In each story I trace the interaction of four key elements: the child, the family, the therapist and the music. The emphasis in each piece of work was slightly different, and I will attempt to portray this both verbally and diagrammatically.

Background

Currently in Britain, it is thought that one in every thousand children has either a life-limiting or life-threatening condition (Mash and Lloyd-Williams 2006). These two categories are defined by the Association for Children's Palliative Care (ACT) in the following way: 'Life-limiting conditions are those for which there is no reasonable hope of cure and from which children and young people will die' (ACT 2007). Included among these conditions are those which cause progressive deterioration and loss of function. Conditions which may be termed life-threatening include those for which 'curative treatment may be feasible but can fail, such as children with cancer' (ACT 2007). In either case, the need for palliative care may become apparent at any time, such care being defined by the World Health Organization (WHO) as 'the active, total care of the child's body, mind and spirit' which they stress 'also involves giving support to the family' (WHO 2007).

The WHO acknowledges the importance of effective multi-agency partnerships for children requiring palliative care. It also underlines the immense value of families being engaged in the care of the child. This is echoed by recent music therapy literature in the field. Lindenfelser (2005) writes about work with terminally ill children, exploring parents' perceptions of music therapy and their responses to it. She comments on the potential for music therapy to 'create a supportive and bonding experience between family members, and improve communication and expression of feelings' (Lindenfelser 2005, p.2). In her article 'Music therapy in children's hospitals' Dun (1999) argues for families' 'active and creative involvement in music therapy as a way in which they may be empowered at a time when they feel that they lack control' (p.63). Other texts endorse the use of music therapy both with the sick child and their family (Aasgaard 2002; Flower 2005; Nall and Everitt 2005; Rees 2005), and, following a child's death, with surviving family members (Mayhew 2005; Rees 2005). In the examples that follow, I want to illustrate what Aldridge (1999, p.24) calls an 'ecology of relationships': different constellations that emerged in the work with these three families.

Alice

Alice was just under two when she started to come for weekly music therapy sessions at a small north London children's charity. She had multiple and complex physical needs, including epilepsy and visual impairment.

Hypotonia meant that keeping her head up was difficult and she was unable to sit without support. She had no development of expressive language. Despite all these difficulties, her mother described her as an 'extremely happy child, always smiling and laughing'. She was most at ease when lying on the floor, rolling to propel herself around a room, encountering objects or toys on her travels.

Although Alice's needs were numerous, my initial anxieties were more concerned with the environment in which this work was going to take place. Having worked predominantly until that time within a school environment, this was a new place of work for me, one which encouraged parents to be present in their child's therapy sessions. Whilst the education context included much liaison and discussion with parents about their child's therapy, I had never previously worked with a parent in the room. I did not know how this would work or how it would affect the work.

Once in the room, however, my anxieties evaporated. Alice was immediately responsive to the musical reflections which I made to her vocal sounds or movements, her voice swooping and her hands brushing the strings of the guitar as she rolled towards it. Our musical interactions seemed purposeful and clear, being built on week by week. Elli, her mother, offered an attentive and warm presence for Alice in the sessions. She provided the physical support Alice needed, and appeared to enjoy the musical relationship which her daughter was eager to develop with me.

This is what Elli says about the music therapy sessions:

> I cannot emphasise enough the importance of music therapy for me and Alice... I had spent so much talking about what Alice couldn't do, it was so refreshing to come and have her able to do something and enjoy it.

I noticed that Elli talked about it being important both for herself and for Alice. It was interesting to consider what it was that had been important to her, given that the focus of the work had seemed to remain so clearly between myself and Alice. Elli's own words perhaps describe more vividly the reason why the sessions had such an impact on her:

> She was not just a disabled child in those sessions, she was free to be herself – a wonderful and extraordinary human being who tried hard at everything she did.

Whilst referring to the benefits of music therapy for Alice herself, something is also being said about the process at work here for the parent. For, by being part of the music therapy experience, a parent bears powerful witness to the vitality and uniqueness of their child's life, whatever their skills, disability or lifespan. The primary musical contact was between the therapist and Alice. Her mother, meanwhile, took up the role of an involved observer. From this position she was able to view her daughter differently. She saw her not just engaged with another person, but eagerly immersing herself in a medium which received and made meaning of the musical gestures she was able to make (see Figure 10.1).

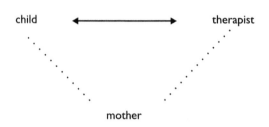

Figure 10.1 The parent as an involved observer

The main focus of the work is between child and therapist, the child being able to make use of the therapist's direct musical responses. The mother plays a supporting role, but remains connected to the events and feelings of the session through the surrounding membrane of the music, and her capacity to enjoy the freedom with which her daughter moves and vocalises.

While this work was developing, we did not yet know that Alice was soon to die. Her death came very unexpectedly when she was just two years and three months old. Amid the grief and loss which followed, their mutual enjoyment of the music therapy sessions acquired a new significance.

Elli's comment that, within music therapy Alice was 'not just a disabled child' signifies how crucial the musical experience is for the child who may be approaching the end of life. As we think of musical responsiveness being one of the infant's earliest experiences, so, too, it seems that it remains available as a means of connection, play and exploration even as death approaches. The chance for the parent to be able to view their child as 'free to be herself' confirms the value of music, not just for the child, but for those around them who witness the quality of that freedom.

Meh-Noor

Whereas Alice's death came unexpectedly, the situation was different with Meh-Noor. She was a six-year-old girl with a particularly aggressive form of cancer. Nearing the end of her life she was being cared for in her own home. Meh-Noor had spent time at the children's hospice at which I worked, and although our days there had never coincided, I had heard that she had been drawn to spending time in the music room. Now, as she neared the end of her life, staff at the hospice suggested that it might be appropriate to visit Meh-Noor and her family at home, a suggestion which appeared to be welcomed by her parents and Meh-Noor herself. So it was that on one hot summer afternoon I found myself standing on the doorstep of a house, carrying a box of instruments and a guitar, unsure what might happen when I rang the bell.

As the door was opened, I was warmly welcomed into a family which was clearly living with dying. As the toddler raced around, and the two older siblings burst in noisily from school, Meh-Noor's mum placed Meh-Noor on the floor, directly in front of me, and in the middle of the room. Her fragility in the face of the noise and activity seemed alarming, and yet her wish to be part of these goings-on seemed strong. While her siblings were swift to lift instruments out of the box, playing them, tussling over them, then discarding them, Meh-Noor moved more cautiously, slowly exploring each object. The music shifted between familiar songs, started by one person and picked up by the others, and improvisations which developed from the songs. It was a vibrant musical happening, full of energy and creativity.

In the bustle of the unfolding music, and the movement of children around the room, Meh-Noor seemed, by virtue of her quietness and stillness to be slightly separate. And yet that quietness and stillness seemed to be an integral part of the family's music as a whole. I was acutely aware that I needed to create harmonic and rhythmic structures which served to hold the lively playing of the family. But, it was also essential that I found a way of responding to the small yet firm musical voice of Meh-Noor. It was as though she was both within the family, and yet also becoming separate from it. The tension seemed almost unbearable to me.

It was striking that this musical happening, which in many ways was so extraordinary, was taking place in such a very ordinary way. The jostling of siblings, the overseeing eyes of parents, the enjoying of songs which held a shared meaning; all were part of a picture of healthy family life, albeit life which contained Meh-Noor's devastating illness. The thoughts of other music therapists are helpful here in considering how shared musical experiences can play a part in supporting the sense of health and normality for both child and family, even within such circumstances.

Aasgaard (2002) describes music therapy with a 14-year-old boy with cancer who had composed his own song. While this boy's physical capabilities were significantly lessened owing to the effects of his illness and its treatment, Aasgaard (2002) describes both the making and performing of the song as 'testimonies of genuine aspects of *health* in this youngster' (p.3). He argues 'that, while absorbed in the musical process, he could be an ordinary teenager, not one primarily identified with a life-threatening illness. Dun (1999, p.62), too, argues that music therapy offers the child who is seriously ill a means of experiencing what she describes as '"the other part" – the healthy self that may be buried under symptoms or feelings of helplessness'.

That demonstration of the 'healthy self' may take the form described above by Aasgaard (2002), but it may also be more fleeting. In describing time with a young child who was very near the end of his life, Rees (2005) describes his unexpected responses, recalling his mother's words of the time: 'Sarah pointed to Alex's feet. "Look" she said, "he's twitching his toes! He does that when he's happy – I haven't seen him do that in a while"' (p.90). The music from the attentive therapist enabled a brief moment of response from Alex, a response taken by his mother to be a sign of his enjoyment and contentment.

It seems as though the possibility of experiencing these moments of vitality are important for both child, parent and the wider family. A musical act of health, however small or brief, bears testimony to the life of the child. It also allows the family the ease and fluency of its own health in the midst of a situation dominated by disease.

By describing families 'participating actively and creatively in music therapy', Dun (1999, p.63) emphasises qualities which are connected more easily with health, life and growth than with our imagined experience of being with the child nearing the end of life. It was something of this active and creative living that seemed so striking in that initial contact with

Meh-Noor's family. Here were a family who were living with the dying of one of their members, but, at least in this instance, were able to meet, play and revel in an animated, health-giving moment in which they seemed to seize the musical experience with thirst and energy. Meh-Noor's brother captures something of this energy in writing afterwards.

> My sister and I came back from school, seeing Meh-Noor, Claire and my father sitting on the floor while my mum was recording Meh-Noor with the instruments. At first I was kinda surprised but after my mum explained what was happening I was excited. Then I was playing the musical instruments. I did enjoy myself a lot.

In this family's shared playing, perhaps it is also possible to see something of what Aasgaard (2002) observes as gifts being both given and received through what he describes as 'musical acts of love'. He describes a child's smile during music therapy as a gift from the child to the parent. The parent's capacity to be musical, perhaps singing or playing with their child, is similarly a gift towards the child. It can signify their wish and capacity to accompany them as far as possible on their journey. Meh-Noor's older sister writes of the way the experience of music therapy became part of a poignant memory.

> Our music sessions with Claire are very memorable... When I saw a gentle, soft smile on Meh-Noor's face it reminded me how hard she had struggled though her illness and how she tried to enjoy the music sessions.

Meh-Noor died at home a week after this meeting. It was a few months after her death that the family invited me to visit them again at home. This prospect made me anxious: I had been so moved by their appetite for contact and connection with me, one other and the music on my first visit. How could that appetite still be there after the death of their child? I couldn't imagine what this meeting would be like.

And then, as the door swung open, there they were, open and warm in their greetings. Mum was briefly tearful as we hugged, but all seemed to want to plunge into, almost devour, a new musical experience. The children of the family seized my box of instruments, and began to play with life and energy, adding to the emerging melée with their own instruments and suggestions for songs. Again, amazingly to me, there is ordinariness to the musical contact, as though here, in this moment, there is health and life.

Yet, gathered in their sitting room again, I felt strongly the space on the floor where Meh-Noor had sat previously. And as the music unfolded, Meh-Noor's absence was felt increasingly, not just through the concrete physical reminder, but also through the missing thread in the musical ensemble. In musical terms, it was as though the sextet had become a quintet, in which all the voices had to mould and adapt their parts, hearing the silence of the missing voice and finding ways to keep the essence of the lost voice in the remaining five.

This one-off session seemed to act as an echo of the one previous session with Meh-Noor. It was as though the past, in which Meh-Noor was focal, had been brought into the present. My offering of music and the bringing of a familiar box of instruments, together with some of the same songs or structures, brought the past into the here-and-now. Rather like the recapitulation section in classical sonata form, a theme or subject introduced at the outset of the work returns, its key elements recognisable and welcome. In being with Meh-Noor's family those key elements were their capacity to embrace the musical experience, weaving health and illness, substance and fragility into their playing. This capacity seemed just as present in the session following her death as when she had been present. But, as they played together now, they brought, as every recapitulation should, not just a straightforward revisiting of the first theme, but also something new or unexpected in their attempts to shift into this new shape. Perhaps it was important that the older siblings now brought out the instruments they were learning at school, as though to bring in the hint of a new theme, their ongoing life and health captured by the display of their new skills.

Being with Meh-Noor's family and working in this way, in a home and in a post-bereavement phase, was a new area for me. It differed, too, from work I had read about. For instance, while Mayhew's (2005) exploration of group work with bereaved siblings is thorough and contributes much to current thinking, it also describes work with a different focus. Although her groups were made up of bereaved siblings from different families, the 'group' which I found myself with was that of the family itself. Here, the absence of the daughter and sister was shared between group members. What was it then that both I and the music could offer this family? How could I think about the role of the therapist in this work?

Figure 10.2 offers a way of understanding the possible layers of relationship and connection within this work. Unlike the sessions with Alice, where the primary focus of relationship was between the therapist and child; here, the primary relationships are those between the family members themselves. The therapist takes a less central position, part of her function being to offer musical equipment, structures and her own musical self, which could be appropriated by the family to underpin the work they themselves were doing. At the same time there are possibilities for moments of direct contact, either musical or verbal, between therapist and different family members, possibilities to which the therapist needs to remain open and alert. In order to respond to these moments, the therapist needs the capacity to shift her focus in a way which matches the shifting, surging patterns of musical relating and feeling in the family around her.

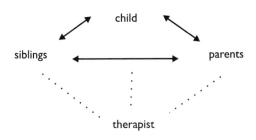

Figure 10.2 Possible layers of relationship and connection with the music therapist

For example, while it was necessary to act musically to match the strong drumbeats of the younger sister, I also needed to respond to the brother's wish to demonstrate the chord progression that he had mastered on the guitar. In our first session, with the animated buzz of musical exploration all around, I needed to hear and reflect in my playing the soft but insistent music Meh-Noor produced. In the meeting following her death, it was also important to manage some moments of thought about her absence, and the space, on the floor and in the music, previously held by her. Moving between these levels required a lively yet solid musical presence, holding structure and flexibility in fine balance. Perhaps that was possible for me in this instance because Meh-Noor's family, through their very open and honest expressions of loss, need and joy, took these musical experiences and used them in such an immediate and affecting way.

This openness of need, and the way in which that might have an impact on the focus of the work, is further defined by the experience of being with Tara and her family.

Tara

With Tara's family a different participation was required of me. She was four months old when she came to the hospice. Her parents moved in as well, having also spent the first few months of her life with her in hospital. She was a beautiful baby being cared for by loving and attentive parents who were working hard to come to terms with the complexity of her medical difficulties and the expected brevity of her life.

When I first met Tara, I sat alongside her cot, watching the rise and fall of her breathing, looking for the smallest of responses as I gently sang her name. As I did so, I was very aware of her mum's presence. We started to talk about Tara and the intricacies of her needs, and mum wondering how music therapy might help her. It was a question I was asking myself. Tara's responses seemed so small that I wondered how a connection between therapist and child might be possible. Then mum asked the simplest yet most poignant question: 'What can I do for my daughter?' And in the moment of that question being voiced, the focus of this whole music therapy encounter shifted. Suddenly, the relationship between therapist and child was of less importance than the need to support and encourage the bond between this mother and her baby.

We thought together about how strong that bond already was; how Tara would have grown so familiar with her mother's voice whilst *in utero*, and how important that voice, together with the familiarity of her mother's feel and smell, would be to her now. Together, we thought about how her mother might hold and sing to Tara, bringing to mind the familiar songs of her own childhood as a resource, and adapting their speed and dynamics to suit Tara's own breathing or state at any one time. Amid the pain and uncertainty of this time, music offered a way in which Tara's mother could connect with her daughter in the most ordinary, and yet unique, mother and baby experience.

In the immediacy of this musical contact between mother and daughter, we see something of how the close previous relationship between an expectant mother and developing foetus was brought into the reality of this unexpected present. The past, with its laying down of communicative and emotional bonds, was now, through the sharing of song, available as an ordinary and yet highly meaningful experience in the present.

Tara's father was a skilled musician, a guitarist who had dreamed of his child becoming a drummer with whom he might play duets. The thought held many hopes and aspirations, not just for the musician his child might become, but also for the quality of relationship they might enjoy in the future. Now though, his daughter's condition meant that this dreamed of future, with all its musical possibilities, needed to be mourned, wrenched from the shape it had taken in his imagination and fitted into an altogether different present.

Following the connection with Tara's mother, my thought with her father was about how his own music might connect him with Tara in this present. I wondered with him about whether it was possible for him to play his guitar. But the thought of bringing it from home seemed too difficult for him, as if it might carry too much meaning.

Offers of support or encouragements for him to play with Tara seemed to need to be very gentle. As I left work one day, I decided simply to leave the hospice guitar in the lounge area outside Tara's room. I didn't make any comment on it to her dad, leaving the instrument as the most indirect offering, which he could then make use of or not, as he felt able.

A few days later, I walked through the hospice lounge, coming to see how Tara was doing, and on rounding the corner stopped abruptly. Dad was sitting by Tara's cot, holding the guitar and playing quietly to her. I moved away quietly, reluctant to insert myself into this musical moment shared between father and daughter. It seemed as though he was mourning many losses, among them the musical future he had imagined sharing with his daughter. But amidst this grieving, he found a way also of seizing and creating a musical present.

The courage with which both Tara's mother and father accepted the many offers of support shown to them at this time was humbling. The way in which we were able to work together helps to demonstrate a further aspect of music therapy practice with families at such difficult times. My direct contact as the music therapist with Tara was limited. This came about because of the need for a different priority in the work.

It seemed, as illustrated in Figure 10.3, that the main focus of the therapist's work here needed to be in offering musical and emotional support and direction to the parents. The crucial relationships were between the three of them, and the role of the therapist was to support them in enjoying the fullest relationships possible in the time that Tara was alive.

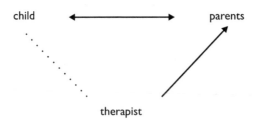

Figure 10.3 The main focus of the therapist's work.

Here again, we see a shift in the therapist's focus, allowing for attention to be given to the very particular needs of the child and family. Those needs differed greatly for the families of Alice, Meh-Noor and Tara, and it was vital for the therapeutic approach to be able to bend and adapt in response to those needs.

Conclusion

While I have proposed in this chapter three different frameworks for thinking about the role of the therapist and the therapeutic approach, these are not intended to be rigid structures. Rather, they have developed from my reflections on the work with these three families, work which has high-lighted the various ways in which families may be able to make use of what music therapy offers.

Music therapy with Alice opened up for me the possibility of working with families in the room. Although the main thread of the work was in the emerging musical relationship between child and therapist, the mother acted as an active observer of that developing relationship, witnessing the fullness with which her daughter was able to connect and communicate until the time she died.

Meh-Noor's family were able to experience moments of healthy, creative family time with her, even in such extraordinary circumstances. The music we shared together after Meh-Noor's death needed to encompass the silence of her absence. Yet, even here, the musical expression had its own moments of vitality, capturing an echo of previous music within the liveliness of its present sounds. Here, the therapist seemed to be an offerer of music, giving the opportunity for a family to meet in their playing, and working to hear and support musical voices as they emerged.

The offering that took place within Tara's family was of a different order again. Here, the therapist's music was largely absent. Instead, the offering was made more directly towards the parents, helping them to be as fully Tara's parents as possible in the short time they knew they had. Through her singing mum offered the voice and presence which Tara would have known innately through the experience of her short life. Through his guitar playing dad found another expression of the tenderness and warmth he felt towards his daughter.

Visiting the family home, while writing this chapter, Meh-Noor's father told me a story. It was a story about a tabla, told to him by his father, himself a virtuoso tabla player. The story goes that when one person sits and plays a beautiful, well-made instrument skilfully, it is possible for other instruments, sitting unplayed in the room, to begin to resonate with the sound of the tabla, its music drawing from their silence an answering echo.

It felt, at the time, as though this story was about more than musical instruments, as though it was a comment on the interconnectedness of human life. It spoke of the deep-seated need for one person to relate to, and resonate with, another. It spoke of dependence, of communication, of family.

Being with, and writing about, these families has demanded from me a willingness to examine both myself and my practice. In this area of work, perhaps more than any other, a flexible approach which can be shaped by the family's needs is crucial. It takes us far beyond the point at which we wonder whether parents or other family members should be a part of a child's therapy. Rather, it leads us to ask how they and we together might be a part of this experience. Music therapy allows the dying child and their family to find ways of resonating and sounding together. I, as therapist, have been privileged to share in the rich possibilities of this musical and human experience.

References

Aasgaard, T. (2002) *Musical Acts of Love in the Care of Severely Ill and Dying Children and their Families*. Music Therapy World. Available at www.musictherapyworld.de/modules/archive/stuff/papers/TrygveLove.doc, accessed on 17 January 2007.

Abad, V. and Edwards, J. (2004) 'Strengthening families: a role for music therapy in contributing to family centred care.' *Australian Journal of Music Therapy 17*, 3–17.

Abad, V. and Williams, K. (2006) 'Early intervention music therapy for adolescent mothers and their children.' *British Journal of Music Therapy 20*, 1, 31–38.

Ainsworth, M.D.S. (1973) 'The development of infant–mother attachment.' *Review of Child Development Research 3*, 1–94.

Aldridge, D. (1999) *Music Therapy Research and Practice in Medicine: From Out of the Silence*. London: Jessica Kingsley Publishers.

Aldridge, D. (2004) *Health, the Individual and Integrated Medicine: Revisiting an Aesthetic of Health Care*. London: Jessica Kingsley Publishers.

Association for Children's Palliative Care (ACT) (2007) *Children's Palliative Care: Descriptions and Definitions*. Available at www.act.org.uk/content/view/10/136, accessed on 18 March 2008.

Austin, D. (2002) 'The Wounded Healer: The Voice of Trauma: A Wounded Healer's Perspective.' In J. Sutton (ed.) *Music, Music Therapy and Trauma*. London: Jessica Kingsley Publishers.

Barnes, G.G. (1998) *Family Therapy in Changing Times*. Basingstoke: Macmillan.

Bick, E. (1963) 'Notes on Infant Observation in Psychoanalytic Training.' In M.H. Williams (ed.) (1987) *Collected Papers of Martha Harris and Esther Bick*. Strathay: Cluny Press.

Biehal, N. (2005) *Working with Adolescents: Supporting Families, Preventing Breakdown*. London: BAAF.

Bion, W. (1962) 'A Theory of Thinking.' In Bion, W. (1967) *Second Thoughts: Selected Papers on Psycho-Analysis*. New York, NY: Aronson.

Bowlby, J. and Ainsworth, M. (1953, 1965) *Childcare and the Growth of Love*. London: Penguin Books.

Bowlby, J. (1988) *A Secure Base: Clinical Applications of Attachment Theory*. London: Routledge.

Brenninkmeyer, F. (2005) 'Assessment of Attachment Difficulties: Psychodiagnostic Measures.' Unpublished paper, 'Attachment in Action' conference, London.

Briere, J. (1992) *Child Abuse Trauma: Theory and Treatment of the Lasting Effects*. Thousand Oaks, CA: Sage Publications.

Bright, R. (1994) *Music Therapy for Grief Counselling: A Training Video with Study Booklet*. Wahroonga, NSW: Music Therapy Enterprises, Australia.

Broach, S., Camgoz, S., Heather, C., Owen, G., Potter, D. and Prior, A. (2003) *Autism: Rights in Reality*. London: National Autistic Society.

Bromley, J., Hare, D., Davison, K. and Emerson, E. (2002) *The Health and Social Care Needs of Families and/or Carers Supporting a Child with Autistic Spectrum Disorders*. Manchester: Manchester Health Authority.

Brown, D., Scheflin, A.W. and Hammond, D.C. (1998) *Memory, Trauma Treatment and the Law*. New York, NY: WW Norton & Co.

Bull, R. and Roberts, C. (2005) 'The Odd Couple: A Model of Co-Working with Non-Music Therapists.' Conference paper. London: British Society for Music Therapy.

Bunt, L. (2002) 'Suzanna's Story.' In L. Bunt and S. Hoskyns (eds) *The Handbook of Music Therapy.* London: Brunner–Routledge.

Cairns, K. (1999) *Surviving Paedophilia.* Stoke on Trent: Trentham Books.

Cairns, K. (2002) *Attachment Trauma and Resilience: Therapeutic Caring for Children.* London: BAAF.

Casement, P. (1985) *On Learning from the Patient.* London: Routledge.

Chazan, S.E. (2003) *Simultaneous Treatment of Parent and Child.* London: Jessica Kingsley Publishers.

Contact a Family (2006) *Factsheet: Fathers.* Available at www.cafamily.org.uk/fathers, accessed on 1 March 2007.

Cozolino, L. (2002) *The Neuroscience of Psychotherapy: Building and Rebuilding the Human Brain.* New York, NY: W.W. Norton & Co.

Daniel, B. and Taylor, J. (2001) *Engaging with Fathers.* London: Jessica Kingsley Publishers.

Darnley-Smith, R. and Patey, H. (2003) *Music Therapy.* London: Sage Publications.

Davies, E. (2005) 'You Ask Me Why I'm Singing; Song-creating with Children at a Child and Family Psychiatric Unit.' In F. Baker and T. Wigram (eds) *Song Writing: Methods, Techniques and Clinical Applications for Music Therapy Clinicians, Educators and Students.* London: Jessica Kingsley Publishers.

Dickman, I. and Gordon, S. (1985) *One Miracle at a Time: How to Get Help for Your Disabled Child – From the Experience of Other Parents.* New York, NY: Simon & Schuster.

De Backer, J. (1993) 'Containment in Music Therapy.' In M. Heal and T. Wigram (eds) *Music Therapy in Health and Education.* London: Jessica Kingsley Publishers.

De Backer, J. and Van Camp, J. (1999) 'Specific Aspects of the Music Therapy Relationship to Psychiatry.' In J. De Backer and T. Wigram (eds) *Clinical Applications of Music Therapy in Psychiatry.* London: Jessica Kingsley Publishers.

Department for Education and Skills (DfES). (2004) *Every Child Matters: Change for Children.* London: DfES.

Department of Education and Skills (DfES) (2006) *National Statistics First Release: Children Looked After in England (Including Adoptions and Care Leavers), 2005–2006.* London: DfES.

Department of Health (DoH) (2004) *Core Document: National Service Framework for Children, Young People and Maternity Services.* London: DoH.

Duhl, F.J., Kantor, D. and Duhl, B.S. (1973) 'Learning Space and Action in Family Therapy: A Primer of Sculpture.' In D. Bloch (ed.) *Techniques of Family Psychotherapy: A Primer.* New York, NY: Grune & Stratton.

Dun, B. (1999) 'Music Therapy in Children's Hospitals.' In D. Aldridge (ed.) *Music Therapy in Palliative Care: New Voices.* London: Jessica Kingsley Publishers.

Fahlberg, V. (1994) *A Child's Journey Through Placement.* London: BAAF.

Fearn, M.C. and O'Connor, R. (2003) 'The whole is greater than the sum of its parts: experiences of co-working as music therapists.' *British Journal of Music Therapy 17,* 2, 67–75.

Figley, C.R. (2002) (ed.) *Treating Compassion Fatigue.* New York, NY: Brunner-Routledge.

Flower, C. (2005) 'When is a Music Therapist not a Music Therapist? An Exploration of Clinical Practice within a Children's Hospice.' Unpublished paper presented at the 11th World Congress of Music Therapy, Brisbane, Australia.

Fosha, D. (2003) 'Experimental Work with Emotion and Relatedness.' In M.F. Solomon and D. Siegel (eds) *Healing Trauma: Attachment, Mind Body and Brain.* New York, NY: W.W. Norton & Co.

Foulkes, S.H. (1964) *Therapeutic Group Analysis.* London: Allen & Unwin.

Frank-Schwebel, A. (2002) 'Trauma and Its Relation to Sound and Music.' In J. Sutton (ed.) *Music, Music Therapy and Trauma: International Perspectives.* London: Jessica Kingsley Publishers.

Gray, D. (2003) 'Gender and coping: the parents of children with high-functioning autism.' *Social Science and Medicine 56,* 631–642.

Haley, J. (1980) *Leaving Home: The Therapy of Disturbed Young People.* New York, NY: McGraw Hill.

Havens, A.C. (2005) *Becoming a Resilient Family: Child Disability and the Family System.* Available at www.indiana.edu/~nca/monographs/17famil.shtml, accessed on 18 March 2008.

Heal, M. (1994) 'An exploration of the emotional impact on co-therapists of running a music therapy group for mothers, their toddlers with Downs syndrome and accompanying siblings.' Unpublished MA thesis, University of East London.

Hirst, M. (2005) *Loving and Living with Traumatised Children.* London: BAAF.

Hodapp, R.M. and Krasner, D.V. (1995). 'Families of children with disabilities: findings from a national sample of eighth-grade students.' *Exceptionality 5*, 32, 71–81.

Howe, D., Brandon, M., Hinings, D. and Schofield, G. (1999) (eds) *Attachment Theory, Child Maltreatment and Family Support.* Basingstoke and New York, NY: Palgrave.

Howe, J. (1994) *Multiple-Family Therapy: A Model For Social Workers At Children's Homes.* Article No. 32. Available at www.multiplefamilygrouptherapy.com, accessed on 13 December 2007.

Howe, D. (2005) *Child Abuse and Neglect: Attachment, Development and Intervention.* Basingstoke and New York, NY: Palgrave Macmillan.

Hughes, T. (2006) 'The Impact of Music Therapy in a Community Setting.' MPhil thesis, Anglia Ruskin University.

James, B. (1996) *Treating Traumatised Children: New Insights and Creative Interventions.* New York, NY: The Free Press.

Jones, A. and Oldfield, A. (1999) 'Sharing Music Therapy Sessions with John.' In J. Hibben (ed.) *Inside Music Therapy: Client Experiences.* Gilsum, NH: Barcelona Publishers.

Keenan, B. (1992) *An Evil Cradling.* London: Vintage.

Kirk, H.D. (1981) *Adoptive Kinship.* Toronto: Butterworth.

Klauber, T. (1998) 'The significance of trauma in work with the parents of severely disturbed children, and its implications for work with parents in general.' *Journal of Child Psychotherapy 24*, 1, 85–107.

Lang, L. and Macinerney, U. (2002) 'A Music Therapy Service in a Post-war Environment.' In J. Sutton (ed.) *Music, Music Therapy and Trauma: International Perspectives.* London: Jessica Kingsley Publishers.

Laqueur, H.P. (1976) 'Multiple Family Therapy.' In P.J. Guerin, Jr. (ed.) *Family Therapy: Theory and Practice.* New York, NY: Gardner Press.

Lindenfelser, K. (2005) *Parents' Voices Supporting Music Therapy within Paediatric Palliative Care.* Voices: A World Forum for Music Therapy. Available at www.voices.no/mainissues/mi40005000194.html, accessed on 6 July 2006.

Malloch, S. (1999/2000) 'Mothers and infants communicative musicality.' *Musicae Scientiae,* Special Issue: *Rhythm, Musical narrative and Origins of Human Communication,* 29–58.

Mash, E. and Lloyd-Williams, M. (2006) 'A survey of services provided by children's hospices in the United Kingdom.' *Support Care Cancer 14,* 1169–1172.

Mayhew, J. (2005) 'A Creative Response to Loss: Developing a Music Therapy Group for Bereaved Siblings.' In M. Pavlicevic (ed.) *Music Therapy in Children's Hospices: Jessie's Fund in Action.* London: Jessica Kingsley Publishers.

Muller, P. and Warwick, A. (1993) 'Autistic Children and Music Therapy: The Effects of Maternal Involvement in Therapy.' In M. Heal and T. Wigram, (eds) *Music therapy in Health and Education.* London: Jessica Kingsley Publishers.

Murray, L. (1992) 'The impact of postnatal depression on infant development.' *Journal of Child Psychology and Psychiatry 33,* 543–561.

Murray, L., Fiori-Cowley, A., Hooper, R. and Cooper, P.J. (1996) 'The impact of postnatal depression and associated adversity on early mother–infant interactions and later infant outcome.' *Child Development 67,* 2512–2526.

Nall, K. and Everitt, E. (2005) 'From Hospice to Home: Music Therapy Outreach.' In M. Pavlicevic (ed.) *Music Therapy in Children's Hospices: Jessie's Fund in Action.* London: Jessica Kingsley Publishers.

National Autistic Society (2006) *The Impact of Autism on the Family.* Available at www.nas.org.uk/nas/jsp/polopoly.jsp?d=307&a=3342, accessed on 10 April 2007.

Nocker-Ribaupierre, M. (1999) 'Premature Birth and Music Therapy.' In T. Wigram and J. de Backer (eds) *Clinical Applications of Music Therapy in Developmental Disability, Paediatrics and Neurology.* London: Jessica Kingsley Publishers.

Nordoff, P. and Robbins, C. (1977) *Creative Music Therapy.* New York, NY: John Day.

O'Gorman, S. (2006) 'The infant's mother: facilitating an experience of infant-directed singing with the mother in mind.' *British Journal of Music Therapy 20,* 1, 22–30.

Oldfield, A. (1992) Video: *Music Therapy at the Child Development Centre, Addenbrooke's NHS Trust, Cambridge.* Anglia Polytechnic University.

Oldfield, A. (1993) 'Music Therapy with Families'. In M. Heal and T. Wigram (eds) *Music Therapy in Health and Education.* London: Jessica Kingsley Publishers.

Oldfield, A. (1994) Video: *Timothy – Music Therapy with a Little Boy who has Asperger Syndrome.* Anglia Polytechnic University.

Oldfield, A. (1999) 'Listening – the First Step towards Communicating through Music.' In B. Carolin and P. Milner (eds) *Time to Listen to Children: Personal and Professional Communication.* London: Routledge.

Oldfield, A. (2000) 'Music Therapy as a Contribution to the Diagnosis made by the Staff Team in Child and Family Psychiatry – An Initial Description of a Methodology.' In T. Wigram (ed.) *Assessment and Evaluation in the Arts Therapies: Art Therapy, Music Therapy and Dramatherapy.* Radlett: Harper House Publications.

Oldfield, A. and Bunce, L. (2001) '"Mummy can play too…" short-term music therapy with mothers and young children.' *British Journal of Music Therapy 15,* 1, 27–36.

Oldfield, A. (2002) Video: *Joshua and Barry: Music Therapy with a Partially Sighted Little Boy with Cerebral Palsy.* Anglia Polytechnic University.

Oldfield, A. (2004) 'Music Therapy with Children on the Autistic Spectrum: Approaches Derived from Clinical Practice and Research.' PhD thesis, Anglia Ruskin University.

Oldfield, A. and Franke, C. (2005) 'Improvised Songs and Stories in Music Therapy Diagnostic Assessments at a Unit for Child and Family Psychiatry – a Music Therapist's and a Psychotherapist's Perspective.' In T.Wigram and F. Baker (eds) *Songwriting, Methods, Techniques and Clinical Applications for Music Therapy Clinicians, Educators and Students.* London: Jessica Kingsley Publishers.

Oldfield, A. (2006a) *Interactive Music Therapy – A Positive Approach: Music Therapy at a Child Development Centre.* London: Jessica Kingsley Publishers.

Oldfield, A. (2006b) *Interactive Music Therapy in Child and Family Psychiatry: Clinical Practice, Research and Teaching.* London: Jessica Kingsley Publishers.

Papousek, H. (1996) 'Musicality in Infancy Research: Biological and Cultural Origins of Early Musicality.' In I. Deliege and J. Sloboda (eds) *Musical Beginnings: Origins and Development of Musical Competence.* New York, NY: Oxford University Press.

Papousek, H. and Papousek, M. (1197) 'Fragile Aspects of Early Social Communication.' In L. Murray and P.J. Cooper (eds) *Postpartum Depression and Child Development.* New York, NY: Guildford Press.

Papousek, M. (1996) 'Intuitive Parenting: A Hidden Source of Musical Stimulation in Infancy.' In I. Deliege and J. Sloboda (eds) *Musical Beginnings: Origins and Development of Musical Competence.* New York, NY: Oxford University Press.

Papp, P. (1983) 'Family choreography.' In P.J. Guerin (ed.) *Family Therapy: Theory and Practice.* New York, NY: Gardner Press.

Pavlicevic, M. (1997) *Music Therapy in Context: Music, Meaning and Relationship.* London: Jessica Kingsley Publishers.

Pavlicevic, M. (2002) 'Fragile Rhythms and Uncertain Listenings: Perspectives from Music Therapy with South African Children.' In J. Sutton (ed.) *Music, Music Therapy and Trauma*. London: Jessica Kingsley Publishers.

Pavlicevic M. (2003) *Groups in Music: Strategies from Music Therapy*. London: Jessica Kingsley Publishers.

Pavlicevic, M. (2005) (ed.) *Music Therapy in Children's Hospices: Jessie's Fund in Action*. London: Jessica Kingsley Publishers.

Pincus, L. and Dare, C. (1978) *Secrets in the Family*. New York, NY: Pantheon.

Prior, V. and Glaser, D. (2006) *Understanding Attachment and Attachment Disorders*. London: Jessica Kingsley Publishers.

Procter, S. (2005) 'Parents, children and their therapists. A collaborative research project examining therapist–parent interactions in a music therapy clinic.' *British Journal of Music Therapy 19*, 2, 45–59.

Raicar, A.M. (2008) *Child-Centred Attachment Therapy: The CcAT Programme*. London: Karnac Books.

Rees, C. (2005) 'Brief Encounters.' In M. Pavlicevic (ed.) *Music Therapy in Children's Hospices: Jessie's Fund in Action*. London: Jessica Kingsley Publishers.

Rutgers, A., Bakermans-Franenburg, M., van Ijzendoorn, M. and Berckelaer-Onnes, I. (2004) 'Autism and attachment: a meta-analytic review.' *Journal of Child Psychology and Psychiatry 45*, 6, 1123–1134.

Satir, V. (1972) *Peoplemaking*. Palo Alto, CA: Science and Behavior Books.

Schore, A.N. (2003) 'Early Relational Trauma, Disorganized Attachment, and the Development of a Predisposition to Violence.' In M.F. Solomon and D. Siegel (eds) *Healing Trauma: Attachment, Mind, Body and Brain*. New York, NY: W.W. Norton & Co.

Seltzer, M., Krauss, M., Orsmond, G.I. and Vestal, C. (2000) 'Families of Adolescents and Adults with Autism: Uncharted Territory.' In L. M. Glidden (ed.) *International Review of Research in Mental Retardation*, volume 23. San Diego, CA: Academic Press.

Sharpley, C.F., Bitsika, V. and Efremidis, B. (1997) 'Influence of gender, parental health, and perceived expertise of assistance upon stress, anxiety, and depression among parents of children with autism.' *Journal of Intellectual and Developmental Disability 22*, 1, 19–28.

Shepperd, R. (2000) 'Individual Treatments for Children and Adolescents with Post-traumatic Stress Disorder: Unlocking Children's Trauma.' In K. N. Dwivedi (ed.) *Post-traumatic Stress Disorder in Children and Adolescents*. London and Philadelphia, PA: Whurr Publishers.

Sheridan, M.P. (1997) *Play in Early Childhood. From Birth to Six Years*. London: Routledge.

Shoemark, H. (2005) 'Infant-directed Singing as a Vehicle for Regulation Rehearsal in the Medically Fragile Full-term Infant.' Keynote speech at the 11th World Congress of Music Therapy, Brisbane, Australia.

Sinason, V. (1992) *Mental Handicap and the Human Condition*. London: Free Association Books.

Smith, L.B. (2007) *Bonding and Attachment: When it Goes Right*. Available at www.attachment.adoption.com/bonding/what-is-attachment.html, accessed on 13 December 2007.

Sobey, K. and Woodcock, J. (1999) 'Psychodynamic Music Therapy: Considerations in Training.' In A. Cattanach (ed.) *Process in the Arts Therapies*. London: Jessica Kingsley Publishers.

Stern, D. (1987) *The Interpersonal World of the Infant*. New York, NY: Basic Books.

Sutton, J. (2002) (ed.) *Music, Music Therapy and Trauma: International Perspectives*. London: Jessica Kingsley Publishers.

Sutton, J. (2004) 'Understanding dissociation and its relationship to self-injury and childhood trauma.' *Counselling and Psychotherapy Journal 15*, 3, 24–27.

Trainor, L., Austin, C. and Desjardins, R. (2000) 'Is infant-directed speech prosody a result of the vocal expression of emotion?' *Psychological Science 11*, 3, 188–195.

Trainor, L. and Desjardins, R. (2002) 'Pitch characteristics of infant-directed speech affect infants' ability to discriminate vowels.' *Psychonomic Bulletin & Review 9*, 2, 335–340.

Trehub, S.E. (2001) 'Musical predispositions in infancy.' *Annals of the New York Academy of Sciences 930*, 1–16.

Trehub, S.E. (2004) 'Maternal Singing and Musical Development in Infancy.' Keynote speech at Music in the Early Years Conference, Northumbria University, Newcastle.

Trevarthen, C. (1999/2000) 'Musicality and the intrinsic motive pulse: evidence from human psychobiology and infant communication.' *Musicae Scientiae*, Special Issue: *Rhythm, Musical Narrative and Origins of Human Communication*, 155–215.

Trevarthen, C. (1993) 'The Function of Emotions in Early Infant Communication and Development.' In J. Nadel and L. Camioni (eds) *New Perspectives in Early Communicative Development.* London: Routledge.

Trevarthen, C. (2004) 'Music, Communication and the Development of Self.' Keynote speech at the Music in the Early Years Conference, Northumbria University, Newcastle.

Warwick, A. (1995) 'Music Therapy in the Education Service: Research with Autistic Children.' In T. Wigram, B. Saperston and R. West (eds) *The Art and Science of Music Therapy: A Handbook.* London: Harwood Academic Publishers.

Winnicott, D.W. (1953) 'Anxiety Associated with Insecurity.' In D.W. Winnicott *Through Pediatrics to Psychoanalysis.* New York, NY: Basic Books.

Winnicott, D. (1964) *The Child, the Family and the Outside World.* Harmondsworth: Penguin Books.

Winnicott, D. (1971) *Playing and Reality.* London: Routledge.

Woodward, A. (2004) 'Music therapy for autistic children and their families: a creative spectrum.' *British Journal of Music Therapy 18*, 1, 8–14.

World Health Organization (WHO) (2007) *Palliative Care WebPage.* Available at www.who.int.cancer/palliative/en, accessed on 20 December 2007.

Yalom, I. (1995) *The Theory and Practice of Group Psychotherapy.* New York, NY: Basic Books.

Useful Websites

- The Fostering Network (www.thefostering.net)
- British Association for Adoption and Fostering (BAAF) (www.baaf.org.uk)

List of Contributors

Rachel Bull MA, PGCE began teaching in special education before becoming a music therapist in 1998. Since then she has worked primarily with children with a range of disabilities in both school and community settings. Currently Deputy Chair of the British Society for Music Therapy, Rachel also lectures on a number of undergraduate degree courses. Her recent work includes establishing an outreach post for Resources for Autism, providing music therapy for children under five and their families at the point of diagnosis.

Emma Davies has worked as a music therapist in Cambridge since 2000. She is currently based at the Croft Unit for Child and Family Psychiatry and at the Paediatric Department, Addenbrookes Hospital. She has set up a variety of family music therapy projects in early years settings and in the community. She has a particular interest in working with children and families, and has written and lectured on the subject in the UK and abroad.

Tiffany Drake (née Hughes) has been the Head Music Therapist at the children's charity, Coram, in London since establishing the service in 2002. She has recently completed her MPhil degree documenting research into the efficacy of community-based music therapy provision and outcomes for children. Previously she has worked in Bosnia-Herzegovina, at the Pavarotti Music Centre, and in Romania for Music as Therapy. She has presented her work internationally and is currently a member of the Executive Committee of the British Society for Music Therapy. Tiffany has a particular interest in music therapy with families with young children experiencing psychological trauma, attachment, emotional and communication difficulties.

Claire Flower has many years' experience as a music therapist in clinical practice, having worked in a range of settings with a wide variety of client groups. She currently works at the Cheyne Child Development Service at the Chelsea and Westminster Hospital in London. As well as teaching and running a supervision practice, she continues to write about and present her work extensively. Claire co-ordinates the musical life of her local church, and has a growing interest in the interactions between theology, music and the community. All of the above she attempts to combine with being married, keeping up with two children and a big dog.

Joy Hasler trained as a music therapist at Bristol in 1993 after working as a music teacher in a special school. For the last 13 years she has developed a specialist creative arts therapy service for adoptive and foster families. She has personal experience of adoption and fostering, and has published and presented papers on music therapy with traumatised children and their families. She is Clinical Director of CATCH-point Consultancy Ltd.

After practising as a social worker **Vince Hesketh** qualified as a family therapist in 1989. Having worked in a social work childcare team he spent seven years in a specialist team dealing with dilemmas arising from sexual abuse. For the last five years he has worked as the family therapist at the Croft Children's Unit in Cambridge. He also runs a small private practice and is an associate lecturer at the Tavistock Clinic, London.

Jasenka Horvat is a senior music therapist and clinical tutor at Nordoff-Robbins MMT training programme. Over the past ten years she has been working as a music therapist with a variety of client groups, predominantly children, and has developed a special clinical and research interest in exploring the field of cultural, social and family contexts within the music therapy process. She regularly gives music therapy-related lectures and workshops, as well as presenting her work both nationally and internationally.

Sarah Howden (née Russell) trained as a music therapist at Anglia Ruskin University in 2001. She currently works in two mainstream primary schools in north London, offering one-to-one, group and family music therapy, primarily to those who have witnessed or been the victim of some highly traumatic event. She also works with children on the autistic spectrum. Sarah would like to thank Judith Nockolds for her invaluable supervision over the past six years.

Helen Loth is a senior lecturer in music therapy and co-ordinator of the Cambridge Music Therapy Clinic at Anglia Ruskin University. She has worked as a music therapist for over 20 years, specialising in the areas of adult mental health and eating disorders. She is also a trained counsellor and works in primary care. Her research projects have included aspects of music therapy training and she is currently investigating the therapeutic uses of gamelan music.

Amelia Oldfield has over 27 years' experience as a music therapist. She works at the Croft Unit for Child and Family Psychiatry and at the Child Development Centre at Addenbrookes Hospital. She also lectures at Anglia Ruskin University, where she co-initiated the two-year MA degree in Music Therapy Training. Amelia has completed four research investigations and a PhD. She has written three books and has also produced six music therapy training videos. She has run workshops and given papers all over Europe and in the USA. She is married with four children and plays clarinet in local chamber music groups in Cambridge, UK.

Nicky O'Neill studied clarinet with Thea King at the Royal College of Music. She then worked as a clarinet teacher and player, before embarking on the Nordoff-Robbins training course in 1990. Currently she works as a music therapist with children with life-threatening conditions and their families at Great Ormond Street Hospital (this is a Nordoff-Robbins outreach position), as well as for Greenwich Teaching and Primary Care Trust and at the Nordoff-Robbins Music Therapy Centre, London. She works extensively with children and their families and is delighted to be part of this book.

Colette Salkeld MA (music therapy) began her working life as a professional clarinet-tist, working as a freelance player with Scottish Opera and Scottish Ballet before taking up the post of Principal Bass Clarinet with Bournemouth Symphony Orchestra. Following this she worked as musical director of the African Children's Choir, working with traumatised children from Uganda, Kenya and Rwanda. This led to Colette training as a music therapist at Anglia Ruskin University, Cambridge. Having worked mainly in schools for children with learning disabilities, four years ago Colette began working for social services, focusing on children with attachment problems. She received her masters degree in 2006, studying the effectiveness of music therapy as a tool to build secure attachment in adopted children. Colette is married with one child and works privately.

Kay Sobey was convener of the MA degree in Music Therapy, at Roehampton University from 1990 until 2005, and she continues to contribute to the teaching of both the music therapy and psychology students there, mainly concerning the usefulness of music therapy with children on the autistic spectrum. She has worked with children across the age range but currently provides sessions for an early years centre with under-fives who have a variety of developmental problems.

Subject Index

Note: Page numbers in
italics refer to figures

adopted children
attachment problems
141–4
music therapy for
144–56
adoptive parents
difficulties faced by
146–8, 164, 166
involvement in music
therapy 144–56
see also carers
antisocial behaviours,
protective mechanism
162–3, 173–4
assessment for music
therapy 148–53
attachment
adopted children 141–4
and attunement 163
lack of in autistic
children 74–7
looked-after teenagers
163–4
reworking patterns of
41–4
attunement 163, 165
autistic children, music
therapy with 71–86

bereavement
and looked-after young
people 162
music therapy for
bereaved families
183–5
bonding, parent–child
basic bonding cycle
74–5
re-establishing 41–4
strengthening 135
see also attachment

Cambridge Mencap 54

carers
role of in therapy
164–5, 167–9, 170,
173–5
see also adoptive parents
CATCH-point, therapy
service 167–75
Child Development Centre,
Addenbrookes General
Hospital 20–1
co-therapy 83–5, 97–8
communication
children with difficulties
in 91–5, 101
infant–parent, restoring
42–3
music as aid to 132–4
community-based music
therapy 37–51
confidence, increase in
following music
therapy 136
controlling behaviour,
dealing with 134
Coram's music therapy
service 38–9
corporate care 160–2
Creative Attachment
Therapy for CHildren
in foster and adoptive
families
(CATCH-point)
167–75
Croft Children's Unit,
Cambridge 122–37
cultural aspects
musical identity in
traumatised families
47–9
parents of
learning-disabled
toddlers 58–9
'curative factors', multiple
family group therapy
59–61

dissociation,
trauma-induced 107
dying children, music
therapy for 178–82

empowerment of families in
parenting role 60,
94–5, 137, 178
enjoyment of music,
importance of 57–8
*Every Child Matters: Change
for Children* (DfES) 44
experimentation, benefit of
group work 61

families
'holding' in groups
80–1
impact of autistic child
on 73–4, 78–9
multiple family therapy
groups 59–61
universality in groups
81–2
see also adoptive parents;
carers; parents
family music therapy
and attachment after
adoption 141–57
development of 11–13
for dying children
177–89
pre-school children
19–36
for traumatised children
and parents 111–18
fathers, including in music
therapy sessions
123–32
feelings
ability to express in
group environment
82
expressing through
music 108, 132–4,
135

Author Index